COST

The Price For Following Jesus

Mike Baker
Studies by Jason Sniff

COST
THE PRICE FOR FOLLOWING JESUS

Unless otherwise indicated, all scripture quotations are from The Holy Bible, English Standard Version® (ESV®). Copyright ©2001 by Crossway Bibles, a division of Good News Publishers. Used by permission. All rights reserved.

Cover Design: Anissa Ortiz, Karen Norris

Video Production Team: David Schertz, Shawn Prokes, Jason Sniff

Editing Team: Sandi Knapp, Sue Taulbee, Sharon Naylor

iUniverse books may be ordered through booksellers or by contacting:

iUniverse
1663 Liberty Drive
Bloomington, IN 47403
www.iuniverse.com
1-800-Authors (1-800-288-4677)

ISBN: 978-1-5320-7522-3 (sc)
ISBN: 978-1-5320-7523-0 (e)

Library of Congress Control Number: 2019906031

Print information available on the last page.

iUniverse rev. date: 06/12/2019

Table of Contents

Weekly video available at eastviewresources.com/cost

COST

Introduction

Few likely understood the allure of and temptations associated with money more than this first century Christ follower. For many years, he had handled currency of all kinds as people came to his corner table near the edge of the market to pay their taxes. Begrudgingly, as Roman soldiers looked on, the peasants of Galilee registered under their family name, reported their income, and gave their fair share of silver. Truth be told, it wasn't fair at all because our friend, like many others of his profession, had learned how to extort these citizens to make a little extra money on the side. Matthew may have been different, but it is likely that he was a thief just like any other Jewish tax collector and therefore paired with "sinners" in the Bible record.

Then one day, a religious teacher stood before him, called him by name, looked him in the eyes, and invited him into his kingdom with the words, "Follow me." In Matthew's mind this may have been the greatest miracle of all. "Why would a religious teacher like Jesus invite me to follow him?", he may have mused. Then questioning further, "What does a tax collector and sinner have to do with the kingdom of God?" In that moment Matthew's entire economy changed. Suddenly he found value in something other than money and the things money can buy. He considered the cost and abruptly left his tax collecting booth and everything he once valued and became a disciple of Jesus Christ. He never looked back.

In the book that bears his name, it seems that Matthew saw the irony of the contrast between his former profession and his unlikely calling. He, more than any other gospel writer, records the "treasure," "money," "value," "riches" and "giving" teachings of Jesus. Another gospel writer named Luke wrote about the time Jesus had challenged the crowds to "count the cost" before following him. But it is Matthew who helps us define the cost for being a disciple of Jesus. To follow him, one must value him above all, treasure relationship with him, and see all resources as stewardship for him. This is the context for this book. "Cost" is a five-week study where together, we will discover the major emphases in the book of Matthew that speak to the cost of being a Christ follower.

First, we will consider the **obstacle** that money and riches can be when it comes to following Jesus. Then we will study Jesus' teaching about what we **treasure** and how that gives us insight into the path our hearts will follow. Next, we will do a spiritual "price check" and talk about the **value** we place on following Jesus. At this point, we will move from conviction to action, being challenged to see all that God has given us as a stewardship that we **invest in** for his kingdom. Finally, we will learn how all of our resources can become one of the highest forms of **worship**. Are you ready to consider the cost?

Let me encourage you to do three things as we consider the cost of discipleship. First, plan on hearing the sermon each week that corresponds to that week's teaching. It's best to do this in person as we all learn together, but you can also access the services live or on demand at www.eastview.church. Second, make sure you read the daily Scriptures and devotions that accompany them. They are designed to take five minutes or less and will enhance and add layers to the week's main teaching. Finally, you will best experience "COST" in the company of other believers and this means participation in a small group, sharing the weekly studies in the back of this book. Please don't skip this important step. Prioritize your time in your current small group. Join a group. Lead a new group. Whatever you do, don't count the cost alone.

Finally, before we begin our consideration of the cost for following Christ, we must begin by noting that no one paid a higher price for us to come close to God than God himself. In a display of incredible benevolence and investment, God so loved the world that **he gave** his only Son. Jesus, God in the flesh, gave his life on a cross so that we could experience relationship with him. Why? There can be only one explanation. God counted the cost, and thought we were worth it. May this book help us value him as much as he values us.

DAY ONE - OBSTACLE

Matthew 19:22-24

---

*"When the young man heard this he went away sorrowful, for he had great possessions. And Jesus said to his disciples, 'Truly, I say to you, **only with difficulty will a rich person enter the kingdom of heaven.** Again, I tell you, it is easier for a camel to go through the eye of a needle than for a rich person to enter the kingdom of God.'"*

Looking back on it now, I can't remember where we got all the stuff. A tire here. Some plywood there. A hula-hoop, a rope, some two-by-fours, concrete blocks, and more were all part of the project. Add a yard with a tree, some hedges, and a fence and you were ready. Ready for what? Well, first I have to give a disclaimer to people who don't know about childhood back in the mid-1900's. During summer breaks, we didn't have computers, cable television, the internet, smart phones, video games, or supervised activities. As I recall, by age twelve most of my friends and I were left alone during the day as our parents went to work... and we lived to tell about it!

This brings me back to the items mentioned above. What would my friends and I do with all of these random objects? Build an obstacle course, of course. Call it boredom or creativity, but I can remember spending hours coming up with a course of impossible obstacles with the idea that after we had constructed it, we would compete to see who could complete it first. Hop on one foot through four rings. Jump over the fence. Swing on the tree branch over the dirt patch underneath it. Walk the wooden board supported by two blocks. Run up the plywood to clear yet another fence.

Hurdle the hedges and roll an old tire to where you started. It's funny, I don't remember actually running through too many of these courses, but we could sure think up things that would make the race harder.

A story from the life of Jesus reveals that obstacles are not just part of childhood play, but that there are also spiritual obstacles in the Christ-following life. The context of our verses for the day comes from an encounter Jesus had with a religious and ambitious young man. He had heard Jesus' teaching about the kingdom of God and, being a man of faith, was compelled to approach the Rabbi. Confidently, he stated his purpose for engaging Jesus, "What do I need to do to get eternal life?" (Matthew 19:16).

It should be pointed out that this man was spiritual according to the Jewish laws of his upbringing. In fact, when Jesus said that keeping the commandments of God was the way into the kingdom, a smile must have spread across his face. He pressed Jesus further, "Which ones, exactly?" And as Jesus listed five of the Ten Commandments and the law to "love your neighbor as yourself", he must have done an internal inventory: "check, check, check". "All of these I have kept. What do I still lack?", he continued. This young man of faith must have been expecting Jesus to open his arms and say, "Welcome to the kingdom." But he didn't.

Instead, Jesus noted the one thing this man did lack. He pointed out the obstacle to this man's desire to follow Jesus. "If you really want to follow me" Jesus responded, "Go sell all you have and give the proceeds to the poor." Wow. Didn't see that coming. Again, this man was thoroughly religious. In our church we would esteem him as a holy person, a man of God, and likely make him a small group or ministry leader. But Jesus knew there was something that stood in the way of his true pursuit of God. This man's wealth was, like the tires, plywood, and hedges of my youth, the obstacle in the way of following Jesus and inheriting eternal life. Sadly, he walked away.

Jesus used this encounter to teach all of his disciples about an obstacle in the earthly experience that hinders our Christ following. And before we get too far into this study about counting the cost, we must address it. Together, we have to acknowledge that "riches" are a significant obstacle to our faith. I think this is a verse that many of us kind of ignore and hope that somehow Jesus doesn't really mean. But if we pay close attention to this story, we must admit that the man who came to Jesus excited about being a part of his kingdom, walked away when he considered the cost.

2

And we should also pay attention to the fact that Jesus didn't chase him down and compromise his challenge. The man walked away. And, Jesus let him! At this point, our savior simply turned to the other followers and told them how difficult it is to enter the kingdom of heaven.

How difficult? It's harder for a rich person to get into the kingdom than it is for a camel going through the eye of a needle. What exactly did Jesus mean by this statement? Well, he may have been using humor to make a point—the visual of a camel trying to squeeze through the eye of an actual sewing needle is pretty funny. Or, he may have been referencing a short gate or door entrance designed for only humans to pass through. Both are possible according to many ancient middle-east scholars. Which is it? I'm not sure. And I'm not sure it matters. Jesus' point is that a camel is big and slow and awkward in lowering its body to a sitting position. To fit this animal through any kind of small opening is difficult.

It's a story about us. We who are rich are the camels trying to fit through the eye of a needle. I say "we" because of my assumption is that most who are reading this book are 21st century Americans, and therefore "rich" by world standards. It's true that some are richer than others, and most don't consider themselves wealthy, but we are. As I have many times, I encourage you to check out where you stand in the world's economy by going to a website called "globalrichlist.com" and punching in your numbers. You will be shocked at just how rich you are. If you find out that you truly are not "rich," consider it a blessing. This is one less obstacle to hinder your walk with Jesus; which brings us back to Jesus' statement about "the rich" in our verses for today.

His closest followers pressed him for an explanation. And here are two quick take-aways from that conversation: **1) Disciples will always give up something up to follow Jesus.** We may not be told to "sell all of your possessions," but Peter does acknowledge "we have left everything..." (v. 27) and Jesus has disciples who will have "left houses" (v. 29). **2) "With God all things are possible"** (v. 26). It's not impossible for God to get a camel through the eye of a needle and by his grace God will cause rich people to enter the kingdom of heaven. Jesus' point is that we should pay attention to our wealth because, like this young man in our story, it can be an obstacle. So, we begin here. There is a cost to following. Let's start counting.

DAY TWO - CHOKE

Matthew 13:22

"As for what was sown among the thorns, this is the one who hears the word, but the cares of the world and the deceitfulness of riches choke the word, and it proves unfruitful."

I live in Illinois, a state known for its rich farming soil. We lead the nation in annual soybean and corn production and we're a major part of our nation's agricultural output. According to my friend Brad Arnold, who has been working in this industry for many years, U.S. farmers planted 170 million acres of corn and soybeans: yielding about 20 billion bushels of grain last year. That's one trillion (yes, with a "t") pounds of food! Such production numbers would have been incomprehensible to Jesus' first century peasant-farmer audience. But there is something that farmers then and now can relate to.

Soil is important, but the fruitful production of crops is highly dependent on the elimination of weeds and pests that choke out the crops farmers are trying to grow. My friend Brad also shared that growers in America spend $10 billion annually to eliminate these hindrances in their fields. Without this, American farmers would harvest 10% less than the crop's full potential. In other words, getting rid of the problems that hinder the growth of the plants in the field proves fruitful for all of us. I think this is what Jesus is getting at with his parable of the sower and the seed.

In this story about how the word grows in the kingdom of God, Jesus speaks of four different types of soil. But for our purposes in this book and this chapter, we'll focus only on the third kind of soil—the soil that contained thorns. In terms that Jesus' audience clearly understood, he states that even good seed, growing among the thorns, will eventually be choked and prevented from growing. But Jesus isn't just giving out farming tips. This story, like all parables, is an earthly story with spiritual meaning. So what exactly are the thorns that prevent the word of God, planted in the hearts and souls of men and women, from growing?

According to Jesus, the thorns in his story represent the cares of the world and the deceitfulness of riches. Again, this is a teaching on riches and money that we must heed. Our Lord says that the deception of riches will choke the word of God that has been sown and is growing in our souls. Some scholars think that this seed sown among the thorns indicates souls that never truly become Christ followers; but I think it can also be true of believers who have the seed of God in them, but do not reach their full potential for bearing fruit in his kingdom.

Could it be that many of us are unhealthy plants that are not reaching the fruitfulness God intended for us because riches are choking out the word in us? Have you ever wondered why your prayers seem to have lost their passion, your worship seems to be shallow, and your participation at church is simply going through the motions? Have you noticed that your time spent reading the Bible has diminished, your willingness to serve has vanished, and your commitment to do what is right has been compromised? Is it possible that there are thorns that are choking out the word of God planted in us? If we are to bear fruit in the kingdom of God, we must identify these thorns that may be growing in the soil of our hearts.

Identify the way riches may be choking your growth.

I believe there are at least three ways the deceitfulness of riches can choke our spiritual formation. First, we are deceived by riches when we believe money can or will solve all our problems. Most of us have thought of an amount of money that we believe would make our lives better. While the actual phrasing may vary, this thinking usually sounds something like, "If only I had (<u>X amount of money</u>), then I could (<u>get to my desired life</u>)." Second, we are also deceived by riches when we believe money will make us happy. We assume that the more money we have, the more possessions we can afford, and that will make us happy. Finally, we are deceived by riches when we believe money will bring us security. This line of thought leads us to believe that if we had a certain sum of money, it would ensure our safety against all of life's challenges.

Unfortunately, all of these deceptions are the thorns that will choke out the word of God in us. The truth is that only Jesus can heal the problems and circumstances of our lives, only he can give us true joy, and only he can give us security that will last forever. If this is true, then like farmers, we must work hard at eliminating the deception of riches from our lives. We should consider some intentional steps to get rid of these spiritual thorns.

Take intentional steps to get rid of these spiritual thorns.

Begin by thinking through or writing down the major challenges and struggles you have in your life and what it would look like if these changed. Now talk to God about these things. Ask him to help supply your daily need, to give you strength to overcome your current circumstances, and to deliver you from the pain of your struggles. Peter tells us to "cast all [our] anxieties on him, because he cares for [us]" (I Peter 5:7).

Next, list the things that make you happy. Anything from sunrises, to coffee, to friends, to laughter—all these and more could be on your list. You'll probably be surprised to notice that the things that bring you joy can't be bought and will require that you slow down a bit. As a spiritual exercise, take note of common advertisements and identify what they are selling to make you happy. Compare that to your joy list. Ask God to give you joy.

Finally, tell God about your biggest fears and insecurities. They may include fear of failure, not having enough saved for retirement, being stuck in a job you hate, or never finding that special someone. As a spiritual exercise, read all of the "do not be afraid" or "fear not" passages in the Bible (google it, or search a Bible app) and note how Jesus overcomes every fear. How has he overcome your fears? Ask him to give you peace.

God has designed each of us to flourish with spiritual fruitfulness in the soil of his kingdom. The seed of the word of God has all the DNA needed for this to happen, but the thorny deceitfulness of riches could prevent it. Like farmers, both then and now, we must pay attention to the weeds. Spend time today in the word and in prayer, asking our gracious father to destroy every hindrance before it chokes out the spiritual growth he offers us.

DAY THREE - ON GUARD

Luke 12:15

"And he said to them, 'Take care, and be on your guard against all covetousness, for one's life does not consist in the abundance of his possessions.'"

Around our house, my wife Sara and I use a one-word question of conviction when the other has expressed a desire to buy something: "Need?" This is our joking and yet pointed response that questions if something is truly a need. This usually follows a statement from Sara like "I need a new pair of black shoes that I can wear on nice occasions." Or after I say, "I need to up my game with some new workout apparel" or "I need a new shirt." Gently (most of the time) these statements and others will elicit the familiar "Need?" The usual response? "Okay, want, not need." This simple practice helps us guard against getting the two mixed up. The truth is that there is not much either of us truly needs.

Jesus spoke the words that we read today because of an all-too familiar dispute about money. It seems that as Jesus was teaching, some guy in the crowd decides that Jesus is someone with spiritual authority who could solve a family inheritance dispute. He actually asks Jesus to tell his brother to give him his fair share of the inheritance (see Luke 12:13). Jesus responds by saying, "I'm not here to be the judge in a small claims court". However, Jesus does take the opportunity to give an important teaching because he detects that this man's issue is not the injustice of his brother, but the subtle sin of covetousness. This is a sin that we still struggle with today—the accumulation of more and more possessions.

This brings us to our scripture for the day. In this simple sentence, Jesus uses two words to demonstrate how great a temptation it is for us to want more and more all the time. First, he says, "take care," using a Greek word ("horao") that literally means "to stare." I don't think the English Standard Version expresses its meaning strongly enough with "take care". I prefer some Bible translations which use more emphatic words like "beware" and "pay attention" to express Jesus' emphasis. To this Jesus adds the Greek word "phulasso" which was used in the first century to describe a night watchman guarding something valuable. In other words, Jesus says we must stay on guard, beware, stare at, and pay attention to. Don't take your eye off this sin! And what sin does he want us to guard against, pay attention to, and beware of? A sin called covetousness. It happens to be one of the Ten Commandments God gave Moses on the mountain ("Thou shalt not covet..." Exodus 20:17) and Jesus is warning against it here. While this may sound like a big church word, it's very simple. When we see the possessions and wealth of others and desire it for ourselves, it is called coveting. The sin of coveting constantly says, "I want more" but growing Christ followers say, "I have enough." The problem is that our culture constantly encourages us to desire, buy, and want what we don't have. Jesus calls us to live counter-culturally by guarding against covetousness. Today consider how you can stay on guard.

Guard against coveting messaging.

Words are important in this battle against covetousness. Our world is filled with words spoken, texted, tweeted and posted. And ultimately, the words we speak, the words spoken to us, and the words that are loudest and most repeated in our culture are often embraced as truth. When it comes to the accumulation of possessions, we can guard against coveting messaging in two tangible ways.

First, we need to identify the words that makes us want more. Most of us hear thousands of advertisements every day that try to convince us that we "need" some product or service. A game I used to play with my own kids and students in my youth ministry when watching television commercials was to ask, "What are they selling and what are they saying will happen to you if you buy it?" This question helps guard against believing the messages that more technology will make us hipper, a new car will make us cooler, and an exercise bike will make us sexier. Try asking yourself these questions and you'll be surprised at what advertisers are causing us to covet.

The other way to guard against the desire for more is to eliminate "I need" statements from our vocabulary when in fact, we don't need anything, yet find ourselves talking about things we want. You may ask someone who can hold you accountable to do the same thing Sara and I do when we question each other about needs versus wants. Admitting that you are saying you "need" something when in fact it is something you "want" is the first step to changing your thinking about the abundance of your possessions. Pray about guarding against coveting messaging, but also…

Guard against coveting practice.

If we are to heed the teaching of Jesus in this area of coveting, we will have to discipline ourselves, with the help of the Holy Spirit, to change our habits as they relate to possessions.

One tangible way to guard against the constant temptation to desire more is to set up a non-accumulation plan. This begins with limiting the number of our possessions. How many shirts, blouses, shoes, purses, hats, tech toys, flat screens, golf clubs, upgraded phones, and cars do we need? Seriously, put a number on the possessions you have and don't allow yourself to surpass that. What you are doing is coming up with a personal "enough" standard. As a simple example, if I say "Five pairs of shoes are all I need," (I'm a guy; a woman's number may be different) then I don't buy a sixth pair of shoes. It's that simple. Some Christians have even fasted from shopping for periods of time. The point is to avoid the practice of buying and buying, and accumulating more and more.

Another way to work against simply storing up more and more belongings is the spiritual practice of giving. In this instance, I'm not talking about the giving of tithes and offerings to your local congregation, although that is certainly important, as we will discover. The giving I'm encouraging here is giving away items of value that are in your possession. This is a simple exercise to develop a non-accumulative attitude. This can be a regular cleaning of your closets to make donation of nice clothes and shoes to places like Good Will or Home Sweet Home mission for those who need clothing. Or it can be as specific as giving something of value to a friend you know would appreciate it. The point is to develop a holy habit of reflexively giving stuff away. The more you practice ridding your life of accumulated goods, the more you'll notice contentment in your life. That is the ultimate guard against abundance—being content with what we have, for when we are content, we are truly rich.

DAY FOUR - LET GO

I Timothy 6:9-10a

"But those who desire to be rich fall into temptation, into a snare, into many senseless and harmful desires that plunge people into ruin and destruction. For the love of money is a root of all kinds of evils."

In the early American frontier, fur traders had a unique way of catching raccoons with a simple trap that played on the animal's inherent curiosity. The trap consisted of a tin can with about six nails driven into it at a downward angle so that the sharp points of the nails left a small opening between them. This can was then firmly secured in a small hole near a stream or creek leaving the top of the can level with the ground. Finally, the trapper would drop some sort of shiny object, often a piece of tin foil, into the bottom of the can and the trap was set.

While this doesn't seem like much of a trap, it was very effective because of the raccoon's natural instincts. Raccoons are scavengers, so as one came to the water in search of food or anything else it might find, it would discover the shiny object in the bottom of the can. Desiring to have the foil (which is pretty useless to a raccoon, by the way) it would reach its paw past the nails, into the can and grasp the silver treasure. Once it had the precious object of its desire, the raccoon would attempt to pull the treasure out, but this was the genius of the trap.

You see, the raccoon could easily reach its paw into the can, but to grasp the object, it had to widen its paw. Then the nails would pierce the raccoon as it tried to bring its paw from the trap. Over and over, the raccoon would try to pull the shiny object out of the tin cup but was prevented from doing so because of the nails. Eventually, the trader would return and find the raccoon trapped. This led to the animal's death. The sad thing, from the raccoon's perspective, is that at any time it could have released the shiny object, shrinking its paw and allowing it to slip easily out of the can. But the allure of and desire for a shiny object literally led to death. The scripture we read a minute ago teaches a similar lesson about riches.

Writing to his son in the faith, Timothy, the apostle Paul teaches Christians then and now about the downward spiral that takes place in our lives when riches are what we desire. He summarizes with a verse that is often misquoted as "money is the root of all evil." But this is not what Paul says at all. Money by itself is harmless; it is the "love of money" that is a root for evil. In the original Greek of this ancient letter, the apostle uses the word "philaguria"—literally "philos" (love of) "haguros" (silver). "Timothy," Paul warns, "tell the members of your congregation that the love of silver, the desire for riches, will lead to a trap that will end in death." It's a progression that he warns against and that we should pay attention to.

It begins with DESIRE.

The desire is to be rich. Everything in our culture encourages this desire. From a young age, we are pushed to make good grades so that we can graduate. Why? So that we can get a good paying job. It's subtle, but the message is clear; the harder you study, the more potential you have to make money. As we settle into our earning years, we are convinced that raises, promotions, and bonuses are worth anything it may take to get them. This is reinforced by such proverbial sayings as; "The early bird gets the worm" and "No rest for the weary." So we get up earlier, work harder, and stay later, sometimes seven days a week. All of this is driven by our desire to be rich.

This desire leads to TEMPTATION.

The prayer that Jesus taught us actually teaches us to say, "Lead us not into temptation" (Matthew 6:13), but a desire for riches leads us to a place we don't want to go. The evil one (Satan/the devil) preys on our desires. When we desire riches, he knows we are susceptible to at least three common temptations.

The first temptation is overworking. If more money is the goal, then work is the means to get it through overtime and promotions. Work is good, but when it becomes an obsession, we're in trouble. The second temptation is the bending or breaking of rules. If more money is the goal, it is easier to justify unreported taxable income, "fixing" the numbers at work, or stealing from others. The third temptation selfishness. If life is all about more and more money, then one will never truly be generous, because giving money away stands in opposition to accumulating one's own wealth. Surely, there are more temptations to be mentioned here, but this is a start. Which of these temptations is the greatest for you?

Falling into temptation leaves us trapped and plunging.

Notice that the phrase is always "falling" into temptation. That's because no one in his or her right mind runs into temptation. We fall into temptation and then find ourselves trapped by it. Two important words stand out as we conclude today's reading. The first is "snare." This word was used specifically for trapping birds in the first century. Just as the silver object attracted the raccoon and led to its capture, the love of money leaves us unable to free ourselves from its allure. The second word is "plunge." This word (bathos) has to do with drowning, with being in over your head, or being under water. This is evident in our culture in many ways, but debt is the most obvious. This desire for riches causes us to buy things we can't afford, which keeps us working to make monthly payments. The majority of Americans are trapped in this cycle and feel as though they are drowning… all because of a desire to be rich.

Ultimately, the way to freedom, for the raccoon literally and for us spiritually, is simple. Let go! Don't hold on to being rich and the money that comes with it. You will avoid "piercing yourself with many pangs" (I Timothy 6:10b). Don't let the nails of riches trap you; instead, let the nails of the cross free you. Desire Jesus, not riches.

DAY FIVE - SATISFIED

Ecclesiastes 5:10

"He who loves money will never be satisfied with money, nor he who loves wealth with his income; this also is a vanity."

As you consider this verse, let me encourage you to make it personal by participating in an easy exercise. The following is a list of statements, including a blank. Based on your age and/or stage of life, fill in the blank on each statement that relates to you. Stop! I know what you're thinking — I'm just going to skim over these statements and get to the teaching below. But please don't skip this. Find the statement (or statements) below that match your situation best and with a pen; actually write a number in the blank. If you don't, it will mess up this day's entire devotion. Ready? Here they are:

- As a high school student, I think $_____ is a lot of money.

- When I graduate from college, I hope to make $_____ a year in my chosen profession.

- If I could just get $_____ in my retirement portfolio, I'd be set for life.

- If my employer would give me a raise of $_____, my life would be so much easier.

- If my spouse made $_____, I could stay home with the kids.

- If I won $____ in the lottery my life would be awesome.

- I'd consider myself rich if I had $____.

- I would move anywhere and take any job for a salary of $____.

- I wish a long-lost relative would leave me an inheritance of $____.

I hope you took some time to think about a number and fill in at least one of the blanks above. Maybe you resonated with three or four of these statements and have several numbers. Take another look at the amount or amounts you wrote down. That's the amount of money that you think is "enough" to make you happy or keep you secure. It's your number for financial satisfaction. There is no right number and yours may vary greatly from others in your small group, your friends, and even your family. I don't know your number, but I can tell you something about it. Whatever you wrote, however high the amount, however outlandish it may seem— according to our Bible teaching for today, it's not enough. And this verse was written by someone who knew what he was talking about.

For thousands of years, most scholars have agreed that King Solomon authored the words we have read today in the Old Testament book of wisdom called Ecclesiastes. This is significant for our verse today, because although Solomon is touted for his wisdom, there was no one (perhaps in the history of the world) who had more wealth than King Solomon. I Kings 4 gives us insight into that wealth by detailing all that it took to feed everyone in his palace operation for just one day. Beginning in verse 22 and following we find that this included over 6,000 liters of flour and 12,000 liters of corn meal. Of course, it's not a king's meal without meat, so every day (every day!) they prepared ten oxen, twenty cows, and a hundred sheep. A few chapters later we find that Solomon's annual income in gold alone was almost 50,000 pounds (666 talents – see I Kings 10:14). I could go on, but the point is that Solomon's actual number is far higher than any hopeful number you may have written down in the blanks above. Still, it wasn't enough.

Late in his life, when he was thought to have written this book, the rich king assessed all his wealth (and everything else in his life) as "vanity." The word "vanity" may be translated as "meaningless" in your Bible. Both are good translations of the Hebrew word "heh' vel" which means "breath," "vapor," or "mist." Solomon uses this word five times in Ecclesiastes 1:2 and it becomes the theme for his entire book, appearing in 29 other verses. For him, money, income, and wealth are just another part of the human reality that appear like a mist and just as quickly vanish. To this ridiculously wealthy king, falling in love with money is pursuing a mist, grasping a vapor, a meaningless endeavor, a vain pursuit, and a complete waste of time. Why? Because when you grasp at a mist, you can never truly hold it.

The love of money is like this mist. We set out to make money and most of us do; from the part time job at the fast food place, to the labor of the construction site, to the creativity of the design studio, to trading on international markets, to making corporate decisions, to teaching students, and more. And for all of these professions we receive some sort of compensation. But although we find some satisfaction in work that contributes to a better world, it is not enough for true fulfillment. And no matter how much money we make, we won't be satisfied. Satisfaction for both Solomon and for us means to be "sated." This is an old word meaning to be filled or complete. Hear the wisdom of Solomon today. He had unlimited financial resources and everything that wealth could buy, but it didn't fill him. He was rich, but he was empty. It was true for him, and it's true for us. In nearly thirty-four years of ministry I've never heard anyone say, "Money fills me." I suspect I never will.

Go back to that number you wrote at the beginning of this chapter. If that fictitious, dream number will not satisfy you, then what will? And what does this say about wealth and our pursuit of it? Count the cost with me today. Are you pursuing a number that constantly changes and is always out of reach or are you resting in some**ONE** who is the same yesterday, today and forever? The truth is that even if you received all the money you listed in the blanks, you would not be satisfied. Only Jesus can fill the blanks in your life because if you have Jesus, you have enough.

DAY SIX - TURN

Hebrews 13:5

"Keep your life free from the love of money, and be content with what you have…"

As we get older, regular visits to the doctor begin to reveal some things about our physical condition that require change. Inevitably, some physician will tell us that we need to lose weight, cut back on sodium, or have less cholesterol in our diets. Eventually, some test will reveal an elevated sugar level or that our blood pressure is higher than it should be. If you are a student or young adult, you may not relate to the challenges that come with growing older, but you will someday. Enjoy good health while you can, because the day will come when a doctor will prescribe medication along with that terrible four-letter word—diet.

We live in a wonderful era of healthcare where medical professionals can manage just about every health issue we have. Yet at some point, we will be asked to get rid of or reduce something in our diet. This is because many medical conditions are a result of what we take into our bodies. So along with prescribing medications, healthcare providers often suggest that we eliminate certain things that we currently enjoy. Heart condition? Lower your cholesterol. Acid reflux? No more coffee. Diabetes? Eliminate sugar. Celiac disease? Bye-bye gluten. Overweight? Cut carbs. This is why our stores and restaurant menus are filled with products labeled "sugar free," "fat free," "sodium free," and "gluten free."

If you are young, keep eating your Twinkies and drinking your Red Bull, but just remember that a wise pastor once told you that the day is coming when you'll have to eliminate those from your diet. Young or old, in this first week of "COST" all of us have been diagnosed with a spiritual condition that will keep us from the kingdom of heaven. Jesus, the Great Physician, has identified a serious "obstacle" to our spiritual health called "riches". Today, the Holy Spirit, in the book of Hebrews, gives a prescription for overcoming this obstacle; keep yourself free from the love of money.

This chapter continues the "love of money" theme; we have already learned from Scripture that the love of money is a trap and will never satisfy us. Today we consider some spiritual disciplines to help *free* ourselves from the love of money. But what does it mean to free ourselves and how do we do it? Actually, these words get a little confusing as we translate from first century Greek to twenty-first century English. The writer of Hebrews penned the words "tropos aphilaguria" with the word "tropos" meaning "a turning." These words together would have been understood as "let the turn be un-silver loving." In other words, to "free ourselves" from the love of money is to continually "turn away" from it altogether. Spend some time praying and thinking today about how you can turn away from the love of money. Here are some suggestions I would offer:

Turn away from putting trust in money.

As we learned earlier, the reason some of us love money is because we think it will offer us security or will protect us in hard circumstances. In other words, our trust is in money. But the context of Hebrews 13:5 is about trusting God and not money. The rest of verse five reminds us of a promise that God made to Joshua in Deuteronomy 31:6; "I will never leave you nor forsake you." Verse six continues the trust theme by quoting Psalm 118:6, "The Lord is my helper; I will not fear; what can man do to me?" Money and riches are the antithesis of these promises. Money cannot be trusted. Money has left us and will leave us again. Money will forsake us and will not respond to our cries for help or solve our problems. Money will not save us in times of need. The obvious prescription is to turn from loving money to loving and trusting God.

Those of you who have known me as your pastor for many years know that I like to use visuals to help me understand and live out my faith. I'm warning you; this suggestion may seem weird, but many remedies that work are strange (e.g. sitting on a tennis ball for sciatic nerve pain—who knew?). I have tried the tennis ball thing and I have practiced the following "turn" discipline as well. This exercise will require two objects—one that represents wealth, like a dollar bill or a credit card, and another that represents God, like a Bible or a small cross. Place the objects next to each other. Look at them. Now consider which one can truly be trusted. No, seriously. Tell each object your greatest financial fears. Think about your biggest challenge or need and consider which would be most helpful. Literally pour out your heart before the symbols of money and Jesus. By now, you probably feel pretty silly—and that's the point. Ask God to help you always see life as clearly as this trust exercise illustrates. Repeat as necessary to turn from the love of money.

Turn away from advertisements.

Another real part of this battle against loving money is to turn from the daily bombardment of advertising in our culture. This is a multi-billion-dollar industry, because it works. This is why companies are willing to pay as much as $5million for a thirty second commercial during the Super Bowl. The goal is to convince you that you need a certain product and then present it in a way that makes buying it irresistible. You don't know that you need a new exercise bike, complete with online trainers to help you complete your workout, until you see the commercial featuring perfectly toned people working out. Then you want it. Next, you're told that the problem with your insomnia is your mattress. You are guaranteed a great night's sleep if you'll just buy their mattress. This is followed by a flashy commercial complete with a catchy song and winsome images of all the relational possibilities that will be yours with the newest smart phone. The best group selfies ever and cinematic-quality video will change your life... if only you purchase this phone. Some have estimated that Americans see 5,000 advertisements every day. This could get expensive! There are two simple questions that I learned several years ago that may help you turn from the temptation of commercials. First ask, "What are they selling?" Follow that with, "What are they promising if I buy their product?" Simply answering these questions honestly and thoughtfully will help keep you from being lured in to loving things that money can buy.

Turn from comparing yourself to others.

Here is one last consideration for turning away from the love of money. Some of our desire for money and all the things money can buy is nothing less than the covetousness Jesus warned about in his ministry and that God earlier decreed in the Ten Commandments (remember "Thou shalt not covet"?). When my boys were teen-agers, they often told me that other parents were buying cars, athletic apparel, video games, and computers for their students. My response to them was often a very tender, "I don't care." I wish I had really meant it! The truth is that most of us feel pressure to keep up with those around us when it comes to getting things for ourselves and our children. But avoid that trap. Make a spiritual commitment never to purchase anything simply because everyone else has it.

The bottom line is that the love of money is real, and it will take intentional prayer and discipline through the Spirit's power to keep it from becoming an obstacle to your faith. Let's take steps today to keep our lives from this harmful love affair.

DAY SEVEN - MINE

Psalm 50:10

"For every beast of the forest is mine, the cattle on a thousand hills."

I'm a Midwest guy. I grew up in Indiana and my wife and I have spent most of our married life in ministries in Kentucky, Illinois, and Missouri. During that time we have driven thousands of miles in these states for ministry obligations, weekend getaways, and family get-togethers. We know Interstates 55, 74, 65, and 44 like the backs of our hands. Sara can pretty much tell you every restaurant, gas station and hotel and the exit number where each is located. Me? Not so much. I usually just ride along as she drives, working on a sermon or writing this chapter, or answering emails.

But there is one thing I always seem to notice—cows grazing in the acres of fields that line the highways throughout the Midwest. My wife can attest to the fact that whenever I see a bunch of cattle grazing on a random hillside, I quote today's verse. "Look Sara," I say as she smiles in anticipation, "those cows belong to God; Psalm 50:10, 'the cattle on a thousand hills are mine.'" I don't know why, but this verse is one of my favorites in the in the whole Bible. Maybe it's because I'm a city boy and cows still fascinate me, or maybe I'm continually amazed by the grandeur of our God. Either way, when we consider the theme of the week, we must conclude that money is no obstacle to the ruler of the universe.

In this Old Testament Psalm (Psalm 50), we find words that would have been used in an ancient courtroom. Words like "speaks and summons" in verse one, and "calls" in verse four indicate an invitation to take the stand. Further, the word "judge" in verses four and six tell us that one party is making a "charge" (v. 21) against another. Finally, the word "testify" in verse seven lets us know that there is a witness. The frightening thing about this legal scene is that God is the witness and judge who is calling his people to the stand to defend the charge he has against them. And the verdict?

The verdict is that although "your burnt offerings are continually before me (v. 8), I will not accept a bull from your house or goats from your folds" (v. 9). But, why God? Don't you want us to give you animal sacrifices? Surprisingly, the answer is "no." Here, God reminds us of just how much he truly owns. He says that he doesn't need the bulls and goats, "For every beast of the forest is mine" (v. 10). "I know all the birds and I see all that moves on the ground" (v. 11). In other words, God is telling us that he has everything. He owns it all. He can take it anytime he wants. I love the declaration our God makes in Psalm 50:12, "If I were hungry, I would not tell you, for the world and it's fullness are MINE."

This leads to the age-old question, "What do you give someone who has everything?" We might ask this about our parents when we are kids, of a spouse when we get older, or of wealthy friends. There are just some people who are hard to give gifts to because they don't NEED anything. This is especially true of "The Mighty One, God the Lord" (v. 1). What do you give to the God who made it all, controls it all, keeps it all, and can take it all anytime he wants? There is only one thing you can give someone who has everything—everything you've got.

The issue with the people on trial in Psalm 50 was that they were giving God animal sacrifices and they thought that these were adequate payment to God and would make him happy. But God doesn't need more animals. What the Lord desires is the heart behind the sacrifice. Sacrifices to God in the Old Testament were designed to be an outward picture of a heart that was completely given over to God. So, when God saw sacrifices being offered but knew that the hearts of those offering them were not devoted to him, he called them to the stand. "I don't want your animals," God declared in judgment, "I want your heart." And it's the same today. God really doesn't want your money. He doesn't need your wealth. He doesn't do fund drives. Everything—all of it—is his and his for the taking, anytime he pleases. And yet he still wants us to give him something; he wants us.

This happens in two ways. First, God wants our thanksgiving. The sacrifice that should accompany any gift to God, whether it's a bull at the temple or a check in the offering at church, is thanksgiving. "Offer to God a sacrifice of thanksgiving" (v. 14). God states his case and says, "The one who offers thanksgiving as his sacrifice glorifies me" (v. 23). When we give to God, we offer whatever it is as a way of saying "thank you." We can never repay God. We can never impress him with the size of our gifts. But we can acknowledge him with grateful hearts in the gifts we bring. If we are thankful when we give, then and only then, does a bull or offering become valuable to God.

Second, God desires that we regularly make sacrifices to him as a sign of our agreement with him. The Bible word is "covenant" and it is always a sacred agreement between two parties. In this case, God is in a covenant with his "faithful ones…by sacrifice" (v. 5). This is an important understanding of our relationship with Jesus and why we give. A covenant always involves God and someone he chooses. It's not a covenant if God gives to us and we don't give back to him. It's not a covenant if we give to him and he doesn't reciprocate. This means that our giving indicates that we are in relationship with God. Again, God doesn't NEED our sacrifices, but he desires them from us because they indicate our part in the relationship with him.

God recalls for his Old Testament people that this covenant was made by sacrifice. We're not sure exactly which special occasion God was referencing. It could be their deliverance from death at the Passover when a lamb was sacrificed to seal the agreement. He may have been reminding them of any number of ceremonial sacrifices made with the people of Israel through Abraham, Moses, David, Joshua, and others. Whatever sacrifice God is pointing back to, it ultimately points forward to the sacrifice of Jesus on the cross for the New Testament people of God. Why do we give? We give because Christ signed a covenant to save us from our sins. He signed it with his blood. The right thing (and always from a heart of gratitude) is to give him all we can in return.

As we've come to the end of our first week of study we have reflected on the riches, treasures, grace, and giving of our God. Every Saturday throughout this study, we will conclude our week of "counting the cost" by considering, acknowledging, reflecting, and meditating on the eternal wealth of our Heavenly Father. So take a few minutes at the end of this week's "obstacle" studies to consider the cost of following Christ with these questions. As you recognize God's greatness, how much do you really value being in relationship with him? In light of his incomparable worth, how much would you give to follow? As you grasp his incredible generosity, how generous should you be? Think and pray about your answers to these questions. Above all, pray for strength so that the wealth God has given you does not become the obstacle that stands in the way of your relationship with him.

DAY EIGHT - TREASURE

Matthew 6:19-21

"Do not lay up for yourselves treasures on earth, where moth and rust destroy and where thieves break in and steal. But lay up for yourselves treasures in heaven, where neither moth nor rust destroys and where thieves do not break in and steal. For where your treasure is, there your heart will be also."

My wife Sara and her two sisters, Steph and Sue, finally did something this Thanksgiving that they had been talking about since their father passed away over two years ago. Before their dad died, Fred had encouraged his family to rummage through hundreds of boxes from years gone by: some of which had been in storage for decades. I mean no disrespect to my father-in-law because he was a humbly great man, but he was a hoarder. Born shortly after the Great Depression and into a poor family, Fred kept and stored things that many would just have thrown away.

To fully understand this family "treasure" hunt, you'll have to picture the narrowest of wooden stairs, steeply descending into a poorly lit, musty, and damp concrete-floored basement with stacks of boxes. Dust covers most everything including the stained, frayed, and taped cardboard containers. If nothing else, the scene reminds you of Jesus' teaching that things laid up on earth will eventually decay, whether by rust, dust, mold or moth. But my point is not the decaying environment; it's what the sisters found inside the boxes that mattered.

Honestly, most of it didn't mean a whole lot to me, but to the daughters, it was treasure. Inside these boxes they discovered their mom's old china, a box of costume jewelry, (a country preacher couldn't afford more than that) some Christmas tree ornaments from their childhood, and some other odds and ends. I was drawn to a few treasures myself. Among them, a collection of some sermon notes from Fred's preaching through his fifty-year ministry, all meticulously handwritten. As a fellow preacher, I recognize these as sacred documents. Throw in some old Bible commentaries and I had struck gold.

Still, Jesus is right. These are earthly treasures and eventually they will all fade away. Maybe Sara and I will pass some of them on to our children, and they to our grandchildren. But, inevitably they will be lost, stolen, decayed, moth-eaten, and ruined. It is the way of "earth treasure," no matter what it may be. It's not that Jesus is anti-treasure. It's just that he wants us to treasure what will last. This is why he says to store up treasure in heaven. This is a truly eternal investment. Whatever you invest in, today's verse teaches that locating our treasure is the same as locating your heart. If your heart is in heaven, your treasure will be in heaven, but if your heart is on earth, your investments will be here instead.

Throughout the years I have noticed that preachers and theologians approach this "treasure" teaching of our Lord from two different angles. Some contend that Jesus is teaching that the **heart follows the treasure.** In other words, if you invest your money in the stock market, you will fall in love with investment wealth. If you invest most of your time in a hobby like fishing or crafts, your heart will move its allegiance toward lures or painting. And if you invest all of your abilities in work, school, athletics, or music; your heart will beat for raises, grades, championships, and hit songs. **What you invest your time, talent, or money in is what your heart will fall in love with.** I'm confident that if you would show me your bank statement, your weekly schedule, and the organizations you belong to, I would be able to assess your heart accurately.

Other Bible students interpret Jesus' teaching differently. They would contend that the **heart comes before the treasure.** In other words, if you fall in love with fine wine and fine clothes, you'll be likely to spend lots of money on Merlot and Michael Kors. If you are passionate about a particular sports team, (Cubs, Cardinals, Bears...Reds anyone?) you will prioritize their schedule on your calendar and make sure you see or attend every game. If your heart beats fast for golf, shopping, travel, or your children's activities; your bank account will reflect spending on those things. ***What your heart falls in love with will be what you invest your time, talent, and money in.*** I'm confident that even a short conversation would reveal to me what you really care about, and it would allow me to predict with reasonable accuracy where you are invested.

So, which is it? Honestly, I think the genius of Jesus' teaching is that it's both. It's like the age-old debate of "which came first, the chicken or the egg?" It doesn't really matter. Either way you have chicken. So it is with "Does your heart guide your treasure, or does your treasure guide your heart?" It doesn't really matter. Either way it's about the heart. We simply cannot divorce our heart's passion from the resources in our possession. They will both end up in the same place. What we need is a heart check, both to learn its true condition and to cooperate with the Holy Spirit to improve our spiritual heart health. Take this simple exam.

Heart check 1: Time.

What do you treasure with your time? Whether you judge by an old-school calendar with squares, or a phone app with reminders, how much of your time is intentionally designated for Jesus and the kingdom of heaven? Not how much should be—how much is? Is Sunday set aside for worship? Does your calendar reflect a week night for small group? Daily time in the Bible? Daily time in prayer? Scheduled time for serving others? If not, what takes up most of your time? Do this heart check often.

Heart check 2: Talent.

What do you treasure with your talent? How are you using your God-given abilities? Maybe God has given you a brilliant mind, lovely singing voice, winsome personality, athletic ability, skilled hands, or caring heart. Whatever your talent, in what ways are you using it for God? What are you doing with your God-given skills that are for Jesus and his kingdom? What are you doing now that will last forever? These questions will help assess your heart's condition.

Heart check 3: Money.

How are you spending your money? What are your top ten monthly expenditures? List them and you will see quite clearly where your heart lies. If you look at your list and think, "My heart doesn't care about these things, and certainly not in this order," then what can you do to change your spending so that it better reflects your heart? If the list accurately measures your heart and you don't like it, what changes can you make to move your heart and wallet to a place that better reflects your faith? There is nothing like a spending inventory to examine your heart's true passions. Do it today.

Check your heart. Check your treasure. They're in the same place. For where your treasure is, there your heart will be also.

DAY NINE - TREASURE A GOOD NAME

Proverbs 22:1

"A good name is to be chosen rather than great riches, and favor is better than silver or gold."

Yesterday we learned that there are two kinds of treasure: the tangible wealth of this world and the eternal wealth of the world to come. The encouragement for Christ followers is to move our hearts from the things of value on earth to the things of value in heaven. But what are the eternal treasures that we need to incline our hearts to seek? This week we will examine some things that scripture teaches have eternal value. We begin with the treasure of a good name.

Our name is one of the few things each of us truly owns. This is pretty amazing since we don't get to choose our names. This is the job of the parents who either birthed us or adopted us. Sometimes parents choose an old family name, ensuring that the name continues on the family tree into another generation. Sometimes our names are given to honor a close friend of our parents, or even a combination of names (my cousin was named "Bobby Sue" after my dad and mom, Bob and Susie). Other parents lean toward giving their children unique, historic, or whimsical names. This is why we know people named Axel, Atticus, River, Lincoln, and Subaru (okay, I made that last one up... but I'll bet there is someone out there who is named after this famous car brand).

Whatever your name, it serves first on the identifying band around your ankle to make sure you don't get mixed up with the other newborns in the hospital. Before long, it becomes the word people say out loud when they want your attention and the one you instantly respond to when you hear it. Then this name becomes your identity on school papers, personal belongings, and official documents like your driver's license. Eventually, your name evolves into much more than an official proof of your existence; it becomes the word that describes your personality, character, and overall being. These recognizable traits sometimes result in people giving us nicknames that further describe who we are or what others think of us.

Today's Bible verse tells us that our name, this identifying word that we carry with us everywhere, is a treasure we should choose over wealth, silver, or gold. Maybe your Bible version translates "a good name is to be chosen" as "a good name is desirable." Either way, the Hebrew word "ba khar'" (which sounds like my last name) means to make a choice or put something to the test. So, this wisdom saying from the inspired word of God is telling us to choose to make our name good, or to keep testing it to make it better. According to this teaching, an investment in our good name is more valuable than choosing gold, silver, or wealth. A good name, *your* good name, is a treasure and something worth investing in today. But how? Well, it begins with a couple of questions and then a few steps of investment.

What does your name stand for?

Say your name aloud. Not too loud; people will look at you weirdly. I know, many of you are thinking, "I'm not saying my name—that's silly." But don't skip this step. Maybe it will be easier if you make your name part of our verse. Read it as "(<u>your name here</u>)'s good name is to be chosen rather than great riches...." As you personalize this verse, think about whether it is a good name or not. In other words, when others say your name, what do they think, and is it good? An honest (and sobering) exercise may be to ask your spouse, children, friends, and those in your small group to tell you what they think when they hear your name. If this is too intense for you, then do a self-assessment by guessing what they might say. What does you name stand for?

What do you want it to stand for?

Once you think you have reasonably and honestly answered the first question, you're ready to proceed. What do you hope your name represents? Hope? Love? Encouragement? Success? Your company or job title? A major accomplishment? Runner? Fisherman? Teacher? Coach? Preacher? Good friend? Something else? What would you like people to think whenever your name is spoken with reference to you? Since this is a daily study of the Bible, hopefully most of us want to have our names associated with Jesus. This could be expressed in many ways, but wouldn't it be nice if the first thing people thought of when our names were mentioned was "Christian," "Christ follower," "spiritual," or even the generic "churchgoer" or "religious"?

Investment steps for a good name worth treasuring.

Whatever your name stands for and whatever you hope it to be, by the grace of God you can invest in a good name today by taking a few intentional steps. Start with this; God knows your name. Just like everyone else recognizes you by your name, so does the creator of the universe. God is intimately aware of who you are. This was dramatically displayed after our Lord had risen from the dead and simply said to his weeping disciple, "Mary." II Timothy 2:19 says, "But God's firm foundation stands, bearing this seal: the Lord knows those who are his...." You have a good name because God knows it.

Next, surrender your name to Jesus and his Spirit. You will only be able to have a "good name" by giving faith and lordship to THE NAME. When we give our lives to Jesus by faith, his good name transforms us from lost to saved, from dead to alive, and from fearful to hopeful. If you haven't given your life to Jesus yet, this is your first step to a good name. If you have surrendered your life to Christ, your cooperation with the Holy Spirit continues to make you into the person God knows you to be. Through spiritual disciplines (e.g., prayer, fasting, journaling, slowing, and Bible intake) the Spirit changes us to look more like Jesus so that our name represents Christ in us.

Finally, live out your eternal reality. In the end, all earthly treasure will fade, but our names will last forever in Jesus. Revelation 20 talks about where believers' names will be written. In verses 12 &15 John tells us that those who are Christians by faith in Jesus will escape judgment because their names are written in the book of life. So, choose a good name now by choosing a life that is surrendered to the lordship of Jesus and shaped by the power of the Holy Spirit. In the end, your eternal identity will be the new name given to you by the King whose name you represented well on earth.

DAY TEN - TREASURE GOD'S WORD

Psalms 119:72

"The law of your mouth is better to me than thousands of gold and silver pieces."

If I challenged you to write about the thing in life you are most passionate about, what or who would you choose to write about? Disclaimer one: Just because you're participating in an all-church study, you don't have to say something about church. I'll direct all of us to consider the spiritual side in just a minute. Disclaimer two: Some of you don't consider yourselves writers, don't like writing, or haven't written anything since high school English class. For the sake of this exercise, let's just say I'm offering you a million dollars to do your very best on this project. Okay?

Now, what could you write most passionately about? Your spouse and years of marriage? Your kids? Your job, career, or occupation? Your favorite sports team (Bears, Cardinals, Cubs, Reds)? Golfing? Fishing? Traveling? Pinterest? Painting? Cooking? Most of you know that my topic would probably be preaching, which leads me to spiritual passions. If we limited this to the spiritual part of your life, what could you passionately describe with pad and pen? Your church? Spiritual leader? Small group? Answered prayer? A miracle you've experienced? The Bible? Whatever your answer, how much do you think you could write about your area of passion? One line? A paragraph? A page? A book?

For the anonymous author of Psalm 119, there is no need to pose the questions I have listed above. This ancient poem is one man's passionate prose about the Word of God and is the longest chapter in our Bible. Writing a stanza for every letter of the Hebrew alphabet and using eight different Hebrew words for the ways God has communicated, this author's heart overflows through his pen about God's words. For 175 verses he tells us that he loves God's word, keeps God's word, hopes in God's word, delights in God's word, longs for God's word, guards God's word, and meditates on God's word. God's commands teach him. God's words light his path. God's promises comfort him, and God's rules are righteous. God's statutes are perfect. I could go on, but space doesn't permit me to tell you everything he thinks about what comes from the mouth of God. Instead, I want us to focus on our verse above and how the author treasures the word of God.

Let's begin by noting that the focus of this verse is **the law** from God's mouth. This specific expression of God's word is "law"—the Hebrew word "Torah" (pronounced "tow' rah") and associated with the law-giver Moses. In the world of our Old Testament brothers and sisters, the law represented all the rules God had given them for living as the people of God. This means that the Torah is as simple and concise as the Ten Commandments and as extensive as the first five books of our Bible, all of which were written by Moses. To this day, Orthodox Jews refer to the books of Genesis, Exodus, Leviticus, Numbers, and Deuteronomy simply as Torah.

This Torah is what the author of Psalm 119:72 is writing about when he says that the "law from your mouth" is more precious than silver and gold. We could paraphrase this verse using the words we are considering this week as, "I treasure the law of your mouth more than money." Our author valued the law. He found wealth in the Ten Commandments handed down on the mountain. His currency was the civic, ritual, and moral laws written on sacred scrolls. He desired the rules that God had given his people. He treasured the Word of God. But what about us?

In the third chapter of II Corinthians, the apostle Paul compares the law of Moses, written on tablets of stone, to the message of Jesus written on tablets of human hearts (see II Corinthians 3:3). Then he makes this observation, "... if the ministry... carved in letters on stone, came with glory... will not the ministry of the Spirit have even more glory..." (II

Corinthians 3:7&8). In other words, the law in Psalm 119 was glorious but the good news of Jesus is even more glorious. So if someone who lived hundreds of years before Jesus treasured the law of God, how much more should we treasure the laws, commandments, and teachings found in the living Word of God—Jesus—and his written words the Bible? The truth is that we probably don't treasure the Bible enough.

Earlier, I asked you to think about the one thing you could write about passionately and then consider how many words you could write about that topic. I hope you considered that question carefully, but now I want to ask you to turn your attention to the written Word of God, the Bible, and treasure it with me for a moment. In Genesis, the Bible tells the story of how God created everything good, including his "very good" creation: mankind. But we sinned and messed the whole thing up, separating us from God and bringing death into our lives. Yet God in his great love promised to send a Savior, Messiah, King who would deliver us from our sins and from death. At just the right time, he sent his son Jesus who died to take away our sins and rose again to take away our death. This same Jesus is preparing a place for us right now and will someday come to take those who trust him as Lord and Savior home to be with him forever.

This is the truth of the written Word of God that points to the living Word of God: Jesus. As Christ followers, this written story is more valuable than silver or gold. So, you know how this devotion ends, right? Spend a few minutes writing down as many words of adoration, praise and worship as you can concerning your relationship with Jesus, and with the Bible that tells his story. Why do you love the Word of God? What does the Word of God mean to you personally? What is your favorite thing about the Word of God? What verses from the Word of God speak to you? How does the Word of God help you in your daily walk?

Take some time with this spiritual practice of writing about God's word. I believe it will help all of us learn to treasure it more than anything else. Begin by answering the questions I posed just above and then let the Spirit guide you as you write. Keep going, you've only got 150 verses to go.

DAY ELEVEN - TREASURE TRUTH IN GIVING

Acts 5:3&4

"Ananias, why has Satan filled your heart to lie to the Holy Spirit and keep back part for yourself part of the proceeds of the land? While it remained unsold, did it not remain your own? And after it was sold, was it not at your disposal? Why is it that you have contrived this deed in your heart? You have not lied to man but to God."

For the first seven years of my ministry, I was an "old school" youth pastor. By "old school" I mean that a youth pastor's responsibilities back in the 1980's covered every program from the nursery through high school. This means that I led worship for first through fifth graders for nearly 350 Sundays. Leading worship for this age group has more to do with expending energy than dispensing good theology as the song about our verse for the day clearly illustrates. Some who grew up in my tradition will recognize it. Sing along. Share it with your small group.

Ananias and Saphira got together to conspire

A plot, to cheat, the church and get ahead.

They knew God's power...didn't fear it,

Tried the cheat the Holy Spirit.

Peter prophesied it and they both dropped dead.

This was just one verse of the song that was followed by the chorus which began, "God loves a cheerful giver, give him all you've got..."

Looking back on it now, I think, "What kind of kids' song was this?" I wonder if kids walked away scared to death of offering time because they didn't want to die in church. Better be cheerful during offering time kids, or you're next! Well, maybe it wasn't the wisest choice for a children's song, but it really is good theology. God loves a cheerful giver, but he also loves a truthful giver.

In the early months and years of the original church as recorded in the book of Acts, we see that these early followers quickly became a community marked by generosity and giving. In Acts, chapter two, "...they were selling their possessions and belongings and distributing the proceeds to all, as any had need" (v. 45). Two chapters later we find "...there was not a needy person among them, for as many as were owners of lands or houses sold them and brought the proceeds... and laid it at the apostles' feet, and it was distributed to each as any had need" (Acts 4:34-35). As an illustration of this generosity, we read the story of Barnabas selling his field and bringing the proceeds as an offering to the apostle-leaders of the church.

The church was buzzing about Barnabas's generosity, as our ancient brother's story was told and retold. The next time the church came together for worship, a guy named Ananias came forward, representing himself and his wife (Sapphira) with a generous offering. However, when giving his testimony about the gift, Ananias (perhaps wanting to "one-up" Barnabas) told the congregation that they also had sold property and brought *all* the proceeds as an offering for the church. Unfortunately, he was lying and by the Holy Spirit's power, Peter knew it and exposed the lie. Three hours later Sapphira came in and told the same lie. And their ending? Well, to quote a famous children's church song, "They both dropped dead."

It's very likely that the monetary gift Ananias and Sapphira put into the offering that morning 2,000 years ago was substantial. Maybe it was as much as several hundred thousand dollars in our currency, but what we learn from them is that the amount of offering never really matters. Let me say it again, the amount of money you give to Jesus and his church DOES NOT MATTER! Remember, God can get all the money in the world, anytime he wants. What matters most to God is the condition of our hearts as we give. He wants generous givers. He wants cheerful givers. But he desires givers who are honest in their giving and that leads to three quick lessons for us about truth in giving.

Be truthful with yourself (motives).

It appears that this first century Christian couple wanted to give but they hadn't fully thought through their motives. Why were they giving the proceeds to their property in the first place? And why were they giving it to the church? Apparently, they were not sincerely giving to help those who were in need and to advance the kingdom through the church. It would seem that they had ulterior motives. Over the years, I have witnessed some motives in my heart and the hearts of those I serve that are not "true giving." "Untrue giving" can be giving to earn God's favor and recognition. False giving can be donating to church out of obligation. Insincere offering can result in donating to a ministry that directly benefits me and/or my family. Before you give, look deep inside your heart and answer this question: "Why am I giving?" Once you answer that question you can move on to the next challenge in giving.

Be truthful with others (not impressing, inspiring).

The next way we can find truth in our giving is by asking ourselves how we hope others will react to our generosity at church. I know the Scripture that says "...do not let your left hand know what your right hand is doing" (Matthew 6:3). Here Jesus encourages us to give in secret. However, a lot of giving is public and that's fine as long as the goal is for our offerings at church to inspire others and not impress them.

Barnabas inspired others through his giving to Jesus and his church. But our couple from today's verse was trying to impress others with their gift. The Bible says to "stir one another up to love and good deeds" (Hebrews 10:24) and I believe that this also applies to giving. So we need to hear stories about generosity to challenge one another. But when impressing others supersedes inspiring them, our gifts become dishonest.

Be truthful with God (he knows anyway).

Finally, and most importantly, our gifts to Jesus and his church require us to be honest with God. Every bank transfer, every dollar placed in a plate, every gift texted or given online is primarily between me and God. Ananias and Sapphira couldn't fool the Holy Spirit and neither can you or I. God knows your heart and he knows why you are giving. The best we can do is to make sure we sincerely give to him because we want to invest in something eternal by advancing his kingdom through his church.

Think about this during the next offering time at church. And be careful; it's a dangerous thing to give an insincere gift to the God of all truth. "Pastor, are you suggesting that I might 'drop dead' for giving a gift that is not true?" Probably not. On the other hand, I can't be sure. I can't imagine that Peter saw this first-century offering judgement coming. I guess the lesson is just to stick with being honest. Whatever we give, may it be a true gift from our hearts to God, to the church, and intended to inspire others to do the same.

DAY TWELVE - TREASURE GENEROSITY

I Timothy 6:17-19

"As for the rich in this present age...They are to do good, to be rich in good works, to be generous and ready to share, thus storing up treasure for themselves as a good foundation for the future, so that they may take hold of that which is truly life."

Our annual Christmas outreach called "Imagine" is about as rich as it gets for this pastor. Of course, the abundance of donations received from our church family to give to those in our community with the greatest need is inspiring. Each year, our church willingly gives away thousands of coats, toys, and boxes of food worth an estimated $250,000. As I walk through the church days ahead of the distribution, I'm moved by the amount of money spent for these gifts, but that's not why we are rich. When I say "Imagine" is a collection of riches, I'm talking about the thousands of good works I witness as I wander through our building thanking volunteers and greeting our visitors with a hug.

Near the café, hosts serve cups of coffee and hot chocolate for strangers who will soon become friends. At a table nearby, another host helps frustrated parents buckle their child into a car seat. Volunteers in our children's rooms color and play games on the floor with grade schoolers. In the hall, a church member walks arm in arm with an elderly lady while new friendships are formed and prayers are offered at tables throughout the building. Behind computer screens, volunteers warmly greet each person by name while a student offers a man from the Congo a free Bible translated into his native French. People of all races, socio-economic levels, spiritual maturity, and ages weave a beautiful tapestry of love and care.

Down the hall, some lovely women (okay, there are some guys, but they're not lovely) wrap gifts with care for children they may never get to meet. Others clean tables and take out trash to keep our facilities clean and welcoming throughout the eight-hour day. In the parking lot, volunteers carry boxes, push grocery carts, hold umbrellas, load trucks, and help with traffic. Upstairs, diapers are changed, babies are rocked, and a lot of Goldfish are eaten (the cracker thingies, not actual goldfish). I could go on, but you get the idea. These and many more good works are multiplied thousands of times during the day. I've never really thought about it before, but during this annual day of service, what we really distribute is not hundreds of thousands of dollars of goods, but hundreds of thousands of acts of love. We are rich…in good deeds.

In our verse today, Paul tutors his young pastor friend Timothy, to encourage those who are rich in his congregation to be rich in another way. Again, he reminds us that riches can be an obstacle to faith ("Don't be haughty or set your hope on riches" [v. 17]), or that our wealth can be invested, and we become even richer in the spiritual sense. "You want treasure?" he asks. "Store up treasure as a good foundation for the future" (v. 19). Specifically, the old apostle teaches that those who have an abundance of money can increase their wealth in three areas: to be rich in good deeds, generous, and ready to share.

Think of good deeds as currency (Be rich in good deeds).

The word "rich" in these verses is the same word (ploutos in the original Greek) that we have looked at already. It literally has to do with overabundance. In other words, to be rich is to have more than you need; and we normally measure this in terms of dollars and cents. If you have "more than enough" for food, clothing, and shelter—by definition you are rich. But what if you and I assessed the value of our current "good deeds" and dedicated ourselves constantly to increasing our good deeds, as if we were depositing them in an eternal savings account? Just for kicks, let's take the words from Scripture literally and consider together just how rich we would be if each good deed had an actual dollar amount attached to it. If every good deed was worth $10, what would your net worth be? What would your weekly income be? Would you be richer in money or deeds?

Live with a generous mindset (Be generous).

The apostle also encourages us to be generous. The idea behind being generous is a willingness to loosen our grip—to let go easily. We could envision this as the difference between clutching a dollar in our hands, tight-fisted, or holding the dollar on the palms of our hands with fingers opened and relaxed. Go ahead and try this simple exercise. Hold a dollar in your hand without grasping it; this is what it means to live with a generous mindset. Just don't do it on a windy day or you'll donate your money whether you want to or not.

Practically, think of the things in your possession right now that you could live without. If it helps, walk around your house, closet, or garage and literally grab some things of value. Now let go. Release your grip on the clothes or items and take them to Good Will or another place that distributes clothing and goods to the under-resourced. Release your grip on something that you have that others in your small group, church, or serving team could use. Just give it to them. Release your grip on the abundance of goods in your cabinets and bring them to the food pantry. Release your grip on the old mower, snow blower, or car and give it to a neighbor who needs it. Literally everything in your possession that can be held onto, can also be released. Do it.

Be ready to share.

Finally, be ready to share. I had a pastor friend who always carried around a $20 bill with the intention of giving it away when God showed him a need. Invariably, he'd run into a single mom who needed gas for her car, or a person in line at the store who needed some extra cash to pay the bill, or co-workers who forgot their wallet or purse at lunch. How can you be ready to share? Think of at least one way and practice it this week. May God bless you as you treasure the generosity he has shown to all of us.

DAY THIRTEEN - TREASURE JESUS

Colossians 2:2-3

"…that their hearts may be encouraged, being knit together in love, to reach all the riches of full assurance of understanding and the knowledge of God's mystery, which is Christ, in whom are hidden all the treasures of wisdom and knowledge."

I began making a list of knowledge and wisdom that is beyond my understanding to share with you as we open this chapter. The list is really long. I began with "rocket science" as something that is likely way beyond my comprehension. After all, we do have a saying, "It's not rocket science," which means that rocket science is hard. Next, I wrote down quantum physics and the theory of relativity (I was actually amazed at the number of big sounding words and ideas I could name). But I couldn't even form a sentence about quantum physics. I actually Googled "theory of relativity." It was so complicated, I couldn't understand it enough to sound intelligent as I make fun of how little I know about it.

I've seen DNA models but I couldn't tell you a thing about molecular structure. There is some understanding and knowledge that is just too big for my preacher brain to understand. Let's be honest, I got lost in high school Algebra… stuck in some story problem about a train heading north at fifteen miles an hour toward a train on another track heading south at 20 miles an hour…the list goes on. There are literally hundreds (thousands?) of concepts, theories, areas of study, sciences, and technologies that I will never comprehend. Unless your last name is Einstein, you can probably relate.

Thankfully, as a pastor, I chose a profession that deals with something far easier to understand—theology. Scratch that. Theology (the study of God) may be the hardest mental endeavor of all. If the things mentioned above are difficult to understand, try wrapping your mind around the pre-existent (eternity past), all-knowing, all-seeing, all-powerful, creator of the universe we know as GOD. Even if there were a book from that popular series, called "God for Dummies," it would be too complex. The Bible says, "Oh, the depth of the riches and wisdom and knowledge of God! How unsearchable are his judgements and how inscrutable his ways!" (Romans 11:33). We will never fully understand God this side of eternity. This brings us to today's verses.

In the middle of an impassioned statement about how he is concerned for the spiritual growth of the Christians in Colossae (and the neighboring town of Laodicea), the apostle Paul writes that he prays for their encouragement, unity, and riches. But it's not the type of riches we normally think of. He's talking about the riches of understanding and knowledge of the mysterious God. Yes, Paul teaches, God is mysterious and beyond understanding, but he has given us a clear view into who he is through the person of Jesus Christ. Earlier in this same letter Paul says (speaking of Jesus), "He is the image of the invisible God" (Colossians 1:15) and "For in him all the fullness of God was pleased to dwell" (Colossians 1:19). The writer of Hebrews describes Jesus this way, "He is the radiance of the glory of God and the exact imprint of his nature..." (Hebrews 1:3). This means that while God is an eternal mystery, we can learn a lot about him because through Jesus he became flesh and blood in order to reveal himself to humankind.

We've been talking about "treasure" in this book and study, and here we find the word again (remember the Greek word "thesaurus"). But the hidden place where all the treasure is kept is in the greatest treasure of all—Jesus Christ. If we are the least bit interested in God and all that he is: unconditional love, eternal life, forgiveness, hope, purpose, and joy; then Christ is the most valuable treasure of all. Specifically, in Jesus Christ is all the wisdom and knowledge of God, so in knowing him we can come closer to understanding the mystery that is God.

Wisdom is the accumulation of life experiences and learning that gives one the ability to interpret circumstances clearly and make right decisions accordingly. This is why most people we deem wise are older in years. One can be wise "for his age" when he is younger, but wisdom takes time. Maybe this is why God is wisest of all—he's been around since before the beginning. He's seen it all. Made it all. Done it all. And it's this God-sized wisdom that caused him to send his son Jesus. What's so wise about sending Jesus? Well, it's what that sending accomplished for each of us.

Consider the wisdom of God in I Corinthians 1:30, "... you are in Christ Jesus, who became to us wisdom from God, righteousness and sanctification and redemption..." The Father, fully aware of how our sinfulness separated us from his holiness, figured out a way to pay for our sin (redemption) and set us apart as holy (sanctification). No human has ever been wise enough to overcome this sin and separation problem to get to God. But in his wisdom, and because of his great love, God rescued us by sending his son to die for our sins and overcome our death by his resurrection. That's wise. But what about the knowledge of God?

Knowledge is not just a recitation of facts but something much deeper. For example, I can give you hundreds of instructions for writing and preaching a good sermon, but that knowledge alone won't make you a good preacher. When it comes to relationships, the principle is the same. I can give you a lot of factual information about my wife Sara; but just reading a fact sheet about her will not mean that you truly know her. In the same way, knowing many things about God (which we can learn by looking at Jesus) pales in comparison to actually knowing God, which can only happen through Jesus. I'd rather know God than know facts about him. And we can know God because of Jesus. In the end, we shall know God for we will see him face to face (see I John 3:2). Until then, we treasure Jesus above all, because he is the deposit of God's riches of knowledge and wisdom for us until that day.

DAY FOURTEEN - YOU ARE TREASURED

Deuteronomy 7:6-8a

"For you are a holy people to the Lord your God. The Lord your God has chosen you to be a people for his treasured possession, out of all the peoples who are on the face of the earth. It was not because you were more in number than any other people that they Lord set his love on you and chose you... but it is because the Lord loves you..."

It's amazing what someone will pay for an item that has no apparent value. But from time to time through the entertainment media or online news feeds, a story will surface of a seemingly unimportant item auctioned off for an unbelievable amount of money. Some high bids make sense because there is consensus on an item's value. These include rare paintings from Van Gogh, unique gems and diamonds, and Stradivarius-made violins. Some items have nostalgic value. These are often sports-related: old baseball cards, hall of fame jerseys, and sports equipment used by legendary athletes are regularly sold for thousands of dollars. Then there are items that fall into the old and/or historic category: bottles of rum from the 1700's, old coins from Ancient Greece, and paintings from obscure Dutch painters. Other "treasures" are simply bizarre, like Winston Churchill's dentures, a piece of wedding cake from Queen Elizabeth's wedding (that was 1947), and even Brittany Spear's hair from when she tried the bald look. I'm not making these things up. Each was sold for a large amount of money.

The items I've mentioned above (and many more) prove the old saying, "One man's trash is another man's treasure." Most of us would probably not pay the price offered for the possessions mentioned above. Why? Because we don't personally hold them to be valuable. Seriously, who wants Brittany Spear's hair or a pair of dentures from a war hero? Not me. On the other hand, most of us have things in our possession that we would not give up or sell for all the money in the world. These articles have value only to us because they represent a special memory, life-circumstance, or relationship that we treasure. An old high school letter jacket, a little league football, and some paintings from Mikey are among my treasures. What about you? What do you value? Take a minute to identify a few things you treasure that probably wouldn't be valuable to anyone else. Go ahead, jot two or three things in the margin. What possessions would you be upset about if your spouse, your mom, or your roommates threw them away or sold them on eBay? The things we list are precious to us, but can't compare to how God sees us.

As we end our week of "treasure talk" that we began with Jesus' teaching about how our treasures and our hearts will always be in the same place, we come to a surprising treasure that reveals the heart of God. Here it is. God values us. Or as our verse says, we are his "treasured possession." These two words are actually just one word in the Hebrew language used in Old Testament times. The word "seg ul la" comes from a word that literally means "to shut up," as in "locking up" something of great value. Like our New Testament word, "thesaurus," it indicates a secure and safe place to keep what we truly value. And of all things in the world God could treasure, his most prized possession is us. He has chosen the Old Testament people of God through his covenant with Abraham and the New Testament followers of Christ through Jesus as the fulfillment of this covenant. Peter confirms this for us in a first century letter to Christians when he writes, "...you are a chosen race, a royal priesthood, a holy nation, a ***people for his own possession***..." (I Peter 2:9, bold italics mine).

All week we have considered what we do with our treasure, but today let's find worth in this incredible reality—God treasures us. In a world of self-doubt, insecurity, low self-worth, and the devaluation of human life; this one reality is the game changer everyone is longing for whether they know it or not.

We want to know that we are valued, and the God of the universe does value us! Consider with me what it means to be a treasure of the Lord Almighty.

A treasure is chosen.

First consider that treasures are chosen. As illustrated above, very few treasures are valued because of their intrinsic worth. Possessions are not valuable in and of themselves. They are only as valuable as someone thinks they are. This verse is amazing because "the Lord God has chosen you...". There is someONE who thinks that you and I are valuable. But we are not treasured because we are valuable, we are valuable because we are treasured by the one who matters most.

A treasure's value is determined by its owner.

Here again, we see that we are "his treasured possession." God has determined that we are valuable. This means we never have to question our value. Just as a family heirloom that has been passed down for generations is a treasure to us; you and I never have to question whether we are treasured. Let me make this incredibly personal for you. You don't have to seek your value from others. You are not treasured as a woman because of your outward beauty and sexual appeal. You are not a treasured guy because you are athletic, muscular, and strong. You are not treasured because you are a wise leader, a smart business person, or a savvy investor. You are not treasured because you made the grades, made the team, or made millions. You are not treasured because of your achievements, your title, or your personality. You are not treasured because of what you can do for others, or what you bring to the table, or the legacy you have left. All of the things that we think make us valuable in the eyes of others have nothing to do with our value in God's eyes. It's this simple. You are valuable because God values you. He made you, loves you, and has a great plan for you. So, stop finding your value in anyone or anything else.

A treasure indicates a place, and our place is the heart of God.

God has "...set his love on you and chosen you..." We began this chapter considering some of the crazy prices people have paid for possessions that seem to be totally worthless, but all this pale in comparison to the price paid for us. Today's verse is not just lip service from a distant God shouting from heaven, "I love you." No, this verse represents the heart of God and his great love for us. His heart is with us, his treasure, and like the two men in the parables, he would give anything to have us. When Jesus walked the earth, he said, "No greater love hath any man than this, that he lay down his life for his friends" (John 15:13, KJV). If you want to know how much God values us, it's easy to find out. Just look at how much he paid. The price God paid for us to be his treasured possession was the life of his Son Jesus on the cross. How valuable we must be!

DAY FIFTEEN- VALUE

Matthew 13:44-46

"The kingdom of heaven is like a treasure hidden in a field, which a man found and covered up. Then in his joy he goes and sells all that he has and buys that field. Again, the kingdom of heaven is like a merchant in search of fine pearls, who on finding one pearl of great value, went and sold all that he had and bought it."

In the era when game shows dominated the morning television schedule, there was probably no more popular show than "The Price is Right." In fact, this show that first aired in 1956 is still in regular production. Those of us who are older remember Bob Barker as the host of this "reality TV" show where contestants are randomly selected from the studio audience to bid on featured items. Younger viewers know that Drew Carey has hosted "The Price is Right" since Barker retired in 2007. But enough game show history. It's what the game is about that gets us to our verse for the day.

The object of the game is to try to guess the actual price of any number of retail items, along with bigger prizes like vacations, cars, and boats. Each item is dramatically presented on stage with models doing that hand-wave-thingy as an announcer with a cool voice describes it in detail, ending with, "All this can be yours if the price is right!" The game begins as smaller items, maybe a set of golf clubs or a microwave oven, are described in detail. One by one, each of four contestants guesses the price of the item in question. The contestant who is closest to the actual price, wins that round.

The funny thing about the show is that some people (mostly guys like me who don't shop much) have no idea what most things cost: blurting out a number way below the actual value. Often, they are so far off from the real cost of the item that the host will laugh, and the crowd will moan. On the other hand, there are people on this show who are obviously savvy shoppers and can guess, almost to the penny, what something costs. These people are more like "the man" and "the merchant" in the two fictional stories Jesus tells us in Matthew 13 to explain the value of the kingdom.

In the first story a man discovers a hidden treasure in a field. The word for treasure here, in the Greek, is the word "thesaurus"— which in Bible times usually indicated the place someone stored valuables— a wooden box or chest. Jesus says the kingdom is like this man who finds the proverbial "hidden treasure." Whose field was the treasure in? How did the man find it? Did he have a permit to be there? Was there video surveillance? We don't know the answer to these questions or any others because these details are not important to Jesus' story. Simply, the man values whatever he has found in this box so much that he sells everything he has to buy that field and gain the treasure in it.

The second story is similar, except that this time a merchant (the word indicates one who travels to buy and sell goods in the marketplace for profit) has found a pearl of great price. Again, Jesus keeps the story simple…he doesn't tell us where the merchant found the pearl…he doesn't tell us how big the pearl is…and he doesn't even talk about how oysters are ceremonially unclean in the Jewish world. Jesus' point is that this man sells everything he has so that he can buy this one incredible pearl. He valued the pearl over everything he owned.

Why did Jesus tell these very short stories? Well, Jesus told parables all the time; it was his way of making theology easy for people like me to understand. The kingdom of God is complex. It's both "here" and "still to come." It's both "eternal" and "here on earth" as it is in heaven. So Jesus explains the kingdom in terms of value. And though some theologians and Bible teachers have interpreted these simple stories in complicated ways, I believe that's unnecessary. Here are the two simple things I think Jesus is trying to say about the kingdom:

1. The kingdom of God is the most valuable thing there is.

Most of us, like the guys in these stories, are looking for what's valuable in this life—what really matters. Some search for it in physical appearance, health, and exercise. Others hope to find it in financial success, security, and investments. The places some search to find value in life are myriad: sports, academic achievement, business growth, promotion, and fame. But the most valuable thing you could ever find in this life is the kingdom of heaven, which is to say, life in Jesus Christ. If you have found Jesus, do you value him like the treasure and the pearl? If you have not found Jesus, what do you think you'd value about him?

2. The great value of the kingdom is worth great sacrifice to get it.

When you discover Jesus and all the earthly and eternal implications associated with becoming a Christ follower, you would give anything to be included. In other words, something of great value is worth great sacrifice. Just as the pearl and field were worth more than all the combined wealth these men had; the kingdom of God is worth more than relationships, money, popularity, earthly possessions, success, comfort, and health. This is, of course, a heart decision one must make daily, sacrificing every earthly desire and resource for the joy of the kingdom. If you have found Jesus, how have you valued him in your life, wealth, and service? If you have not found Jesus, what would you give for all the things he promises? As you think about the value and the cost of the kingdom, maybe it would help to see it differently.

What if God miraculously appeared to you in a dream tonight and promised to heal your pain, forgive your past, give you purpose and belonging, and guarantee life forever; and then put a price tag on it. How much would you pay? Seriously, if God told you all this could be yours if you paid him $100,000, what would you sell to pay it? What if he sweetened the deal to $250,000 and said he would let you and all your family members into the kingdom of heaven? Beyond that, what would you give for an orphan, a widow, or an under-resourced person here at home or throughout the world? If you could pay for friends and neighbors and strangers you have empathy for; would you try to save millions of dollars to pay their way into the kingdom as well? Just how much would you pay if God put a literal, monetary price tag on human salvation?

Well, he did. The price God set for his kingdom to come to earth, the kingdom that would save all mankind from all the sins they had ever committed, was the blood of a perfect sacrifice. That's an incredibly high price in anyone's value system. But the price is not the incredible part of this story. What's incredible is that instead of charging us for the value of our salvation, he paid it through the death of his son on the cross so that he could give it to us for free. Grace like this is the greatest thing we could ever discover and warrants our everything in return. All he asks is that we love him with our heart, soul, mind and strength, and accept the gift from him that we could never afford to buy: the free gift of eternal life.

DAY SIXTEEN - IMMEDIATE GRATIFICATION

Hebrews 12:16 & 17

"[See to it] ... that no one is sexually immoral or unholy like Esau, who sold his birthright for a single meal. For you know that afterward, when he desired to inherit the blessing, he was rejected, for he found no chance to repent though he sought it with tears."

In the early, youth ministry days of my pastoral calling, there were many things that truly amazed me. Looking back, I can't believe how God used a guy who was equally passionate and disorganized to encourage so many students in their faith. Abundant grace was coupled with people around me like my wife Sara and super-star youth volunteers like Dale and Lori Lowe in Lexington, Kentucky, and Val and J.R. Hoyer in Kissimmee, Florida. Equally impressive was the ability for inspired teens to change the entire trajectory of their lives as they felt led by the Spirit. I am still impressed with how quickly students will go "all in" when compared to the adults I know. I could go on relating the ways junior and high school students impress me most. But, one much less spiritual thing cannot go unmentioned.

I still stand amazed at the appetite teen-aged boys have for pizza. From time to time, I would treat my small group of young men to an all-you-can-eat pizza buffet. All I can say is that I usually said a prayer for the restaurant. Back in the day, you could find a noon buffet for $5.99. My guys may have shut down dozens of pizza joints. Guys don't select pizza. They stalk it. They attack the pizza like prey in the wild. I've seen high school boys pile their plates seven pieces high, all the while grazing with a breadstick wrapped in another piece. This is before the "I'll bet you can't eat 12 more slices" challenges begin. Of course, the spiritual victories in youth ministry outweigh everything else, and yet I would still say that the appetite displayed by guys eating pizza is nothing short of miraculous. And while appetite is entertaining, even if not admirable, it can also be devastating.

This is the case with the Old Testament Bible character, Esau. He was the older twin brother of Jacob, sons of Isaac and Rebekah. The incident referenced in today's verse is found in Genesis 25:29-34. It will help to understand that Esau was a "man's man" and his brother Jacob was a "mama's boy". These twins couldn't have been more different. Esau was described as hairy—an athletic hunter who preferred the great outdoors. Jacob is described as a quiet man—a soft, indoor kinda guy who obviously knew his way around the kitchen.

And so, the story goes that on one particular day Esau had been out hunting in the fields since dawn. He was tired and hungry from stalking and chasing prey, apparently with no success. On the other hand, Jacob had been cooking stew all day, and as the red beans (lentils) simmered over the open fire, the smell filled Esau's nostrils and he had to have some. Right now! And this is where the deceiving Jacob sees his opportunity. He offers a bowl of stew to his brother with a huge "if." **If** you give me your birthright, I'll let you have some stew. The birthright in the Old Testament was the privileged inheritance of the firstborn son that not only gave him a double portion of his father's estate, but also full authority in the family. There was no way Esau would trade all of his future for a bowl of beans! But he did, and thereby became a biblical example of a value system gone wrong.

As we consider the things of value in our lives, we must ask whether we value immediate gratification or long-term reward. The Bible warning today is clear "See to it…that no one… is like Esau." In other words, Christ followers are no less likely than Esau to sell their spiritual birthright as children of God to gratify the intense appetite of the flesh. In the context of these verses, we're talking about sex. The writer of Hebrews may have a broader context in mind, but there is no doubt he is associating the very physical appetite for food with that of sex. I think we can agree that sexual temptation is all around us, inviting us to indulge our appetites like an all-you-can-eat pizza buffet or a bowl of stew. But God is warning us not to be like Esau. But how? Consider these three simple steps that may keep us from giving up our inheritance for a simple meal.

Identify the hunger.

Esau was hungry. That's it. Any food would have taken care of his famished state. Surely his mom was preparing the evening meal. His dad had lots of sheep and goats. Esau could have killed a goat or drunk some goat milk for nourishment. He wasn't hungry specifically for his brother's stew, but it was easy, and it was there. We are sexual beings. Like being hungry, most of us desire sex. But what we're really hungry for is the incredible intimacy that comes with someone we love, trust, and are committed to. The sexuality of this world becomes the quick-fix bowl of stew that brings instant gratification but does not satisfy our deepest hunger for relationship. This is why God created sex for marriage between a man and woman and he created us to have an appetite for this sexuality. Unfortunately, there are many options for sex that can never satisfy our appetite for love and intimacy.

Avoid the stew.

After you realize that it is only God's perfect plan for intimacy that will satisfy your hunger, avoid the stew. We don't know Jacob's intentions; maybe he was innocently making stew and took advantage of the moment, or maybe he was setting his brother up. Either way, if Esau hadn't seen, smelled, and salivated over the stew, he wouldn't have been tempted to eat it. Unlike Jacob, we do know the intentions of this culture that consistently presents sexual immorality to humans who obviously have an appetite for sex. The challenge for us is to avoid these temptations. I know, I know; it's everywhere. I am aware that sexuality seems to be everywhere but let me tell you where it's not. It's not on your phone or computer when you decide to be accountable to your spouse, children, parents or friends. It's not in the office or on business trips when you avoid sexual humor and situations. It's not on the television screen that doesn't have that channel. The truth is, there are steps we can take to avoid unholy sex. What ones will you take today? Tell someone. You won't be likely to eat the stew if you don't see the stew.

Don't get so hungry you can't think clearly.

One last thought on this. Esau had let himself get to the point where his physical hunger outweighed his spiritual resolve. I wonder when he last prayed or considered the covenant God had made with his grandfather Abraham and father Isaac? In the same way, regular prayer and Bible reading is the best defense against giving in to our physical appetites as we stay spiritually full. Fill up on the bread of life, and the food of the world will have less allure. Along with this, keep healthy relationships with Christian brothers and sisters. This emotional nourishment may influence our sexuality more than anything else. Find your worth in the life of the church, as a part of something bigger than yourself, and keep yourself emotionally full. Finally, if you are in a healthy marriage, sex is designed to keep you physically satisfied with your spouse so that you will not be tempted by the menu of sexual choices around you. This is biblical (I Corinthians 7:1-5) and is yet another blessing God has given us.

In the end, all sexuality that doesn't align with God's plan for marriage will ultimately end up being a disastrous decision that fills an immediate need but jeopardizes an eternal inheritance. Consider Esau today and ask God to help you value the promise more than the impulse.

DAY SEVENTEEN - COUNT THE COST

Luke 14:28-30

"For which of you, desiring to build a tower, does not first sit down and count the cost, whether he has enough to complete it? Otherwise when he has laid a foundation and is not able to finish, all who see it begin to mock him saying, 'This man began to build and was not able to finish'".

One of the ways this preacher unwinds on a Sunday night is by watching a couple of shows on the HGTV network called "Beach Front Bargain Hunt" and "Island Life" with my wife, Sara. Usually, after I get home from preaching at our evening service, we'll settle in with some popcorn or leftover Sunday lunch and spend the next two hours home shopping with other people's money. Why? There's not a much better mindless wind down than watching other people buy homes on the beach and honestly, after a long day of preaching, I consider moving to the tropics every Sunday night. I'm just kidding about the moving part, but Sara and I do escape for couple of hours nearly every week via strangers who have decided to move to a warmer climate.

If you haven't seen the show, it begins with prospective home buyers who have an initial meeting with a real estate agent. Usually, over drinks at an outdoor waterfront restaurant, these couples describe the kind of house they are looking for. This conversation includes "must haves" and "wants" and covers such things as the desired number of bathrooms and bedrooms, views to the ocean, access to the water, and style of home. This goes on for a few minutes until the agent gets down to business with the question, "How much are you willing to spend for all of this?" Sometimes the amount given is decidedly lower than the average price for the housing market they are in. It's at this point that the realtor shares the bad news, "It will be difficult for you to get the type of house you're looking for at that price. Would you be willing to look at some homes that don't meet all of your criteria?" In other words, many people know exactly what kind of beach house they want, but they have not counted the cost.

Believe it or not, according to Jesus in Luke 14, purchasing a place on the water and following Jesus have this one thing in common: they both will cost you. And so, as you consider each, you have to answer several questions. What is the value? How valuable is it to me? Will it hold its value? How much do I have? How much am I willing to spend? Will I be able to pay for this? These questions and many more are involved when someone counts the cost. And it is this phrase that came from the lips of Jesus that we must consider today. Of course, the crowds following Jesus were mostly poor farmers, craftsmen, and fishermen, so they weren't in the market for beach front property on the shores of Galilee. But they could relate to the building of a tower.

When you hear the word "tower," your mind may immediately go to some ancient castle in Europe complete with moats and drawbridges, but Jesus was talking about another kind of tower. It was common in Jesus' day for the owner of a vineyard to build a simple structure on the corner or in the middle of his property for surveillance of his crop and for protection from theft. With perhaps a smile on his face and a twinkle in his eye, Jesus pokes fun, "Can you imagine a wealthy land owner starting a tower and then not having the resources to finish it?" How embarrassing to have half a tower! More seriously, how crazy would it be for a king to charge into battle without assessing both his and his enemy's army? That would be more than embarrassing; it would be deadly. Jesus' advice for tower builders, army leaders, and would-be Christ followers is the same. First, count the cost. Let's consider two questions to help us understand this teaching.

Who was he talking to?

Luke 14:25 tells us that great crowds were following Jesus. While most rabbis, pastors, teachers, and leaders might have touted these great numbers as a measure of success, Jesus challenged those who were following. You see, he knew that the kind of following they were currently engaged in didn't cost them anything. They followed because Jesus' words were inspirational and entertaining. They followed because they or a loved one had been healed or were seeking healing. They followed because he had provided tangible needs like bread (the feeding of the five thousand). They followed because they wanted to be on the winning team (the promised Messiah was here). For these original and literal Christ followers, it was easy and beneficial to be a "disciple." But Jesus knew that it would eventually cost them.

He literally stopped the Jesus parade and described the cost of following him. Simply, it would cost relationships (Luke 14:26), all that one had (Luke 14:33), and even one's own life (Luke 14:27) to be a disciple of his. I'll bet a lot of people dropped out of his church that day. These were probably good people. They probably loved God and were hoping that God would deliver them. They sincerely loved what Jesus stood for and who he was. They wanted to be a part of this movement that clearly was from God. What about me and you? We love and follow Jesus for many of the same reasons. But there is more to following Jesus than what's in it for us.

What is his point, then and now?

There is a cost to following, according to our Lord, and we have to "count" it. The word he uses here for "counting" is a word (too hard to pronounce even in English) that has to do with small pebbles used for calculating. Picture someone sitting at a table with a pile of small stones pushing each one aside as they count, "one, two, three...." This is how Jesus says we should consider the price of following him. On one hand, calculate the pebbles that represent following as the blessings of freely receiving forgiveness of sin, living and walking in the truth, experiencing the unconditional love of God, having eternal life in him, and truly belonging to his family. On the other hand, we must consider what it costs: 1). He insists on being our number one relationship. He will not be second. 2). He insists on being more important than our possessions. All that we have is from him and for him. 3). He insists on us valuing him over life itself. We must give up this temporary life for the eternal one to come.

Before you take one more step—count, weigh, consider. Think about it. As the realtor always asks, "How much are you willing to spend?" This is how much you value following Jesus. I hope you, like me and millions of others throughout history, will decide that Jesus is worth it. Let's count the cost together and then give all that we have to follow the one who has given it all for us.

DAY EIGHTEEN - A VALUABLE OFFERING

II Samuel 24:22-24

"Then Araunah said to David, 'Let my lord the king take and offer up what seems good to him. Here are the oxen for the burnt offering and threshing sledges and yokes of the oxen for the wood. All this, O king, Araunah gives to the king.' And Araunah said to the king, 'May the Lord your God accept you.' But the king said to Araunah, 'No but I will buy it from you for a price. I will not offer burnt offerings to the Lord my God that cost me nothing.'"

It's called "re-gifting." It is the convenient; yet extremely tacky practice of taking a gift that you have previously received and giving it to someone else. This happens most at Christmas time (at least that's what I've heard). In the rush of parties, shopping, and gift exchanges, we invariably end up with an item we didn't ask for, don't want, and can't return for a full refund. Conveniently, we switch the tag and carry it to the next gift exchange. We have done our duty. We gave a gift. And, if it's worthless enough, it may be re-gifted several times before reaching its final destination. Most of us have done this, but re-gifting is one of the most insincere kinds of giving there is. In fact, it is not giving at all.

I want to make a distinction here between a "re-gift" and extending generosity with what you have been given. For example, a newlywed couple who receives two toasters as wedding presents and gives one of them away to a friend is technically re-gifting. (Do people even get toasters anymore, or do they just order toasted bread from Amazon?) Another example of "acceptable" re-gifting could be buying dinner for friends with a restaurant gift card you received from someone else. You technically didn't pay for dinner, but by sharing, you "paid it forward" as we say. One of the most spiritual moments I ever personally witnessed was from an impoverished kid in the Dominican Republic who shared the bag of M&M's he had just received from a friend of mine. After receiving this rare gift, the boy promptly opened the bag and offered the candy to his friends, one "M" (singular of M&M's) at a time, keeping only one for himself. This kind of giving and other examples like it are technically re-gifting, but the heart attitude behind it is totally different.

Today's Bible verses are part of another story found in the Old Testament that will help us understand our giving, especially as it relates to our giving to God. King David's burnt offering comes at the end of the story and as a result of his own sin. Chapter twenty-four of the prophet Samuel's second letter (I'd recommend that you read the whole chapter) gives us the details. At some point near the end of his life, firmly established in Jerusalem, David decided to take a census. Apparently this was a sin. We're not sure exactly how he sinned by doing this, though we get a hint through Joab's question, "Why does the king delight in this thing?" (II Samuel 24:3). It could be that late in his life, David's pride and desire for personal glory prompted this census. Because of this lack of trust and arrogance, God punished David and his people with a severe plague.

Slowly, and in a way that we don't fully understand, an angel of God carried out the deadly pestilence by killing 70,000 people from the north to the south of Israel ("...from Dan to Beersheba..." – II Samuel 24:15). But as the angel neared Jerusalem, God told his messenger to stop: "It is enough; now stay your hand" (II Samuel 24:16a). David was actually an eyewitness to this angel's stopping point, a hill near the property and threshing floor of Araunah the Jebusite. In this moment, Gad the prophet came to David and gave him a word from the Lord. The king was to build an altar on this threshing floor to make atonement for his sin and for the sins of the people of God. And so, David approached Araunah's house and this is where we observe two valuable offerings that teach us, all these years later, about offerings and value.

First, we see the generous offer of Araunah. All we are told about him is that he is a Jebusite. The Jebusites were the original inhabitants of Jerusalem, so we can infer from this story that at some point, this man (and likely other outsiders) was given grace and allowed to live in Jerusalem along with the people of God. He likely had this land because King David had given it to him, or let him keep it, and so when David approaches, he bows in reverence. Then he offers a gift. He offers to give David his threshing floor (David had offered to buy it) and to give him everything he needed for the sacrifice, including the oxen, threshing sledges, and yokes. That may not sound like much of an offering to those of us who don't understand ancient farming methods, but this is a very valuable offer.

The lesson here is that this Jebusite is giving back to a king who has given him all that he has. As we mentioned, when this man offered his land as a gift and his animals for sacrifice, he was paying homage to the king, who at the least allowed him to live in the land his family once owned, and at the most spared his life during the capture of this city. Again, we are reminded that when we give to Jesus' church and its mission to make disciples, we are returning what we value to the King of Kings who has given us everything. True offerings are directed to our king when, like Araunah, we give out of reverence and worship, and with a willing heart, pay thanks to our king for how he has spared our lives.

The second generous thing we see in this story is how David responds after he has heard his subject's well-intentioned offer. Instead of accepting this incredible gift, the king insists on paying the fair price for the threshing floor and using his own animals for the burnt offering. His reason is one of the most inspirational verses in Scripture on giving: "I will not offer burnt offerings to the Lord that **cost me nothing**." In fact, both men were offering a gift that cost them. Araunah was offering that place where he processed his harvest, along with the tools for growing crops (oxen, yokes, threshing sledges). He was giving up his livelihood. David knew that a true offering to God must cost something. Both valued the cost of sacrifice.

Let's learn from this. Any offering we bring before God is not truly an offering if it doesn't cost us something. If we are just giving God leftovers, or money that doesn't matter to us, and if our tithes and offerings don't reflect some sacrifice on our part, then it is not truly a sacrifice that we are making. Perhaps, this one question will help you as you pray and think

DAY NINETEEN - VALUED PLACE IN THE KINGDOM

Luke 19:8

"And Zacchaeus stood and said to the Lord, 'Behold, Lord, the half of my goods I give to the poor. And if I have defrauded anyone of anything, I restore it fourfold.' And Jesus said to him, 'Today salvation has come to this house, since he also is a son of Abraham.'"

One of the great things about growing up in the church is the number of children's songs that I can still recall nearly five decades later. Songs like "Father Abraham," "In right, out right, up right, down right, happy all the time," "Hallelu – Hallelu – Hallelu – Hallelujah," "I'm in the Lord's army," "If you're happy and you know it," and "I am a C – I am a CH – I am a CHRISTIAN" were all designed to teach Bible truths as well as work the energy out of the kids who were singing them. Of course, some told stories straight from the Bible: songs like "Ten men went to spy on Canaan" and my all time favorite, "Zacchaeus was a wee little man".

Zacchaeus was a wee little man
And a wee little man was he
He climbed up in a sycamore tree
For the Lord he wanted to see

And as the Savior passed that way

He looked up in the tree
And he said, Zacchaeus you come down
For I'm going to your house today

While the lyrics are simple, they pretty much tell the story exactly as Luke does in the nineteenth chapter of his gospel. It is yet another story from the life of Jesus that reveals his purpose for coming. In fact, at the end of the Zacchaeus story, Jesus says, "...the Son of Man came to seek and save the lost" (Luke 19:10). Zacchaeus was lost, even though he was rich. Like the apostle Matthew, he had become wealthy by cheating his own people as a tax collector for the Roman government. He was hated and shunned by his Jewish neighbors and labeled a sinner. But he, like all Jews, was waiting for a Messiah and so when the man that many were calling "the Christ" came to Jericho, he wanted to see him.

It must have been quite a parade with crowds lining the streets, pushing and shoving to catch a glimpse of Jesus. But there was no way Zacchaeus was going to try to mingle with the people who hated him, and he couldn't see over the crowd because of his short stature (thus the "wee little man" description in the children's song). So, he ran ahead along the parade route and climbed a tree for a better vantage point. This is where the story gets interesting because as Zacchaeus thrills at the spectacle of seeing Jesus, the Savior stops right under the tree he is sitting in. I would imagine that Zacchaeus was thinking, "Don't look up, don't look up, don't look up." But because Jesus was looking for him, that didn't work. He called to Zacchaeus by name and then invited himself to his house. This is where the song from my childhood ended, but the best was yet to come.

Something happened during that meal. This is one of the many Bible conversations I would have loved to witness. Of course, the shocked Zacchaeus was the consummate host. He brought out the best cheese, bread, fruits, wine, and likely killed the fatted calf in honor of his holy guest. But somewhere between "Would you like some more bread, Master?" and "Can I have one of my servants wash your feet?", Jesus took control of the conversation. "Tell me about yourself Zacchaeus." One thing led to another and suddenly Zacchaeus was a different man. The presence and power of Jesus in his life had changed him from a greedy tax collector into a generous "son of Abraham." By grace, Jesus had "saved" him ("Today salvation...[Greek "sodzo"—to rescue or save]...has come to this house") and challenged him to change because of his new faith.

We may never know the actual conversation of that day, but we can tell that the heart of this tax collector changed on that day because of how Zacchaeus' behavior changed. He started by giving away half of his goods to the poor. Then he went back through his financial records and noted every time he had cheated to make a profit. His new commitment? He would refund that amount fourfold. I think that there were two astounding results in Jericho that day. First, there were a lot of impoverished people who experienced the generosity of Zacchaeus' changed life when he started handing out money. And second, Zacchaeus enjoyed a closeness to God that he had never experienced before.

Today, let's put ourselves in Zacchaeus' place. The old preaching quip is that Zacchaeus was "up a tree" and "out on a limb" and really, aren't we all? We may not be publicly ostracized as Zacchaeus was, but when it comes to living a perfect life, we are outsiders to God because we all fall short of his glory. Because of the sins we have committed we are all hoping to catch a glimpse of Jesus, wondering if he'll notice us and praying that he can save us and make us a part of his kingdom. So, what if Jesus stopped under your tree today and told you he was coming to your house? Go ahead, imagine it. And then pray your way through these two questions.

What would the dinner conversation be about? After you prayed the best prayer of your life to impress the Savior, what would he want to talk about? Certainly, he would tell you how much he loved you, but beyond that, what would he tell you he came to save you from?

How would you respond as a result of that conversation? What after-dinner speech would you give to Jesus in the presence of all your guests? What would you gladly give away and what would you do to make amends for people you've hurt? Thank God that he invited himself to your house when he came to earth and that for those who welcome him in by faith, we are a part of his kingdom. Value that place in the kingdom. This is the lesson from Zacchaeus.

DAY TWENTY - RISK THAT'S WORTH IT

Matthew 27:57-60a

"When it was evening, there came a rich man from Arimathea, named Joseph, who also was a disciple of Jesus. He went to Pilate and asked for the body of Jesus. Then Pilate ordered it to be given to him. And Joseph took the body and wrapped it in a clean linen shroud and laid it in his own new tomb which he had cut in the rock."

Every week we celebrate the body and blood of Jesus Christ in a sacrament called "communion" or "the Lord's supper." This ceremony of remembering Jesus' death on the cross has been celebrated by Christians for over 2,000 years in a variety of ways. This meal of remembrance started as an actual meal called the Passover meal and there is evidence that in the early church this tradition continued (I Corinthians 11:20-22) as a fellowship meal that eventually came to be known in the church as "love feasts" (Jude 1:12). Over the years, most Christian traditions started including it as a part of the corporate worship experience with a variety of ways to partake.

Some use real bread and a common cup. Others dip bread into the cup (this is called "intinction" which has nothing to do with this chapter, but I like the word). Still others pass trays with anything from broken pie crust, to matza crackers (since they are unleavened like the Passover bread would have been) or whatever form of bread is most convenient. Our church's tradition now celebrates this important rite with tiny cracker squares and small cups of grape juice that every member can easily hold. In fact, a few years back we made the passing of the emblems a little easier by stacking two tiny cups – one with the small cracker and the other with the juice. As the trays are passed, each Christ follower can easily take the cups and hold them until we take communion together as a church family. Normally, I remove the cracker to hold in my hand and this practice led to a very unique communion experience that will get us to our verse for today.

One particular Sunday, I tipped the cup to retrieve the cracker, but it was stuck to the bottom of the cup. Somehow, the juice from the top cup had spilled into the bread cup, making it just soggy enough to adhere to the cup. I stuck my finger in the cup and that's when I noticed something that made communion very real for me. Without being gross, I noticed that the consistency, feel, and look of the soggy, square piece of cracker in my hand seemed like a piece of skin. In that moment, the bread that clung to my finger like a callous or a blister made the body of Christ come alive to me in a way that I had never experienced. It was as if I was actually getting ready to partake of the body of Christ that was broken for me on a cross all those years ago. And as I meditated on the reality of our Lord's sacrifice, my mind drifted to the man in our scripture from today, Joseph.

As far as I can tell, there are only two people who actually held the broken body of Jesus following his grisly crucifixion. There are famous paintings and movie scenes that picture Jesus' mother, Mary, holding Jesus' dead body beneath the cross as only a mother would do, but there is no biblical evidence that this took place. However, all of the gospels mention a man named Joseph of Arimathea who requested the dead body of Jesus from the governor, Pontius Pilate. Most often, the bodies of criminals who were crucified by Rome were thrown into a common grave—piled onto the bodies of those previously executed. But history tells us of this man, unknown until this point of the Jesus story, who was granted permission to take possession of the deceased Jesus. He and his friend Nicodemus actually handled and cared for the broken body of Jesus.

I would encourage you to read all of the gospel accounts of Jesus' burial to learn more about this obscure man named Joseph. Along with today's verses, you can find Joseph's story in Mark 15:42-46, Luke 23:50-54, and John 19:38-42. Though we never hear of him again in Scripture, we can put together a pretty complete picture of this man through these accounts. He was from an as-yet undiscovered town of Arimathea. Up to this point, he was a secret follower of Jesus because he was a member of the ruling Jewish council known as the Sanhedrin. Luke tells us that he was a good and righteous man. John tells us that his fellow Pharisee Nicodemus (you remember him from John 3) helped him prepare the body for burial. And we know that Joseph placed Jesus in his own, brand-new tomb that was in a garden not far from the scene of the cross.

All of this was risky in three ways for a man like Joseph. The first risk was in requesting Jesus' body from the Roman governor. Most of Jesus' followers had scattered when he was arrested, fearing that association with Jesus would mean death for them as well. But Joseph boldly reveals his allegiance to Jesus with his request. The second risk for this man was his reputation among the other Jewish leaders who had condemned Jesus to death. In essence, Joseph put his religious position in peril in order to minister to Jesus as he did. The third risk was being ceremonially unclean because of his contact with a dead body. This disqualified him from all Passover festival participation. Joseph traded the celebration of the year for the menial work of burying the Savior.

As severe as these penalties were, Joseph valued Jesus over the potential consequences and sacrifices. This is an example of someone who willingly used his wealth and position to serve Christ. This obscure Bible character is an example for us and is someone that we should prayerfully emulate today. What would you willingly risk because you value Jesus more? Unfortunately, this one act of devotion is the only thing we know about Joseph. He is never mentioned in Scripture again. But we can imagine that he was there on the first day of the church in Acts 2 and joyfully celebrated many communion meals with his fellow believers. And while others remembered Christ by holding the bread in their hands, Joseph remembered what the body of Christ actually felt like as he tenderly prepared him and placed him in the tomb. It was a valuable experience that he would never forget.

DAY TWENTY-ONE - TRADING PLACES

II Corinthians 8:9

"For you know the grace of our Lord Jesus Christ, that though he was rich, yet for your sake he became poor, so that you by his poverty might become rich."

If you've spent much time in the large cities of this country or the world, you've probably been approached by someone who has asked you for money. In my travels, near and far, I have met children begging for pesos, "untouchables" in the train station extending hands for Indian rupees, and homeless veterans shaking a cup on the street corner, hoping for spare change. In my home town of Indianapolis, I know some people who have sought this form of charity every day in the same spot on the sidewalk for years. To tell the truth, I struggle in all of these situations because as a Christ follower, my desire is to be generous with all that God has given me. Yet I know that my few dollars will probably perpetuate the dangerous lifestyle of panhandling or, worse still, be used for the drugs and alcohol that are often connected with homelessness. I truly wish I could do more, and so I wrestle with my response.

Not much has changed since Bible times. The city of Corinth, the home of the Christians who first read today's verse, was a sprawling metropolis in the first century. Picture New York City with togas and sandals. Because of the city's position between two major seaports, it was a global crossroads. Travelers from the Roman west to the Persian east converged in this city located on the Isthmus of Greece. They came for the entertainment, enjoying both the Olympic-style games (the Isthmian Games) in the stadium and performances of all kinds in the theaters. They came as shoppers, strolling through the expansive, outdoor shopping malls that boasted the unique leather and ceramics made only in Corinth. They came to admire the architecture and worship at the impressive temples to Roman gods. They came to engage in sexual activity with the temple prostitutes (history tells us they numbered 1,000) in "worship" of the goddess Aphrodite.

The result of all this city's commerce, popularity, and population was the vast divide between the rich and the poor. Corinth boasted an elite upper class who lived in palatial estates complete with marble courtyards and gardens. The wealthy dined daily on the finest foods, dressed in scarlet and purple, and relaxed in the shade by their pools. Meanwhile at the other end of the economic spectrum, and in another part of town, the market places were filled with impoverished beggars sitting on mats at every corner, hoping for some Roman coins to get them through the day. Their voices filled the Corinthian air with the constant cacophony of "alms for the poor." Remember, the word for rich means "an abundance" or "more than enough," but the word for poor in these verses is pretty descriptive. It is the Greek word *ptokos* and its root word means "to crouch," as in the bent-over position of a beggar asking for money. The apostle Paul uses this contrast between rich and poor to make a point about the grace of Jesus.

As a member of the pre-existent triune God of the universe, Jesus was rich. As we learned on day seven of this study, God literally has the resources of the entire cosmos at his disposal. We get excited about streets of gold, but that's just pavement to him. He can throw stars—not the ancient oriental weapons—real stars. He can make new stars or new galaxies if he wants to. He can paint the sky at sunset and dawn exactly as he chooses. God's petting zoo includes every creature in the world; his work room covers the endless heavens; his tools are thunder and lighting, snow, hail and rain, and the earth is his footstool. He is rich.

When we compare our resources with God's wealth, we are the poor, crouching in the rags and filth of our sin and death. With lowered heads, we extend a hand God's way, longing for his spare change. We beg for a little mercy, a little hope, some leftover love. Thankfully, God has decided not to give us what we ask for. He doesn't "wish he could do more" as I do; instead, he went to drastic measures to change our circumstances. Jesus, though he was rich, through the incarnation became poor.

Imagine that instead of giving some change from your pocket or a few bills from your purse to the poor sitting on the pavement, you offer to trade places. What if you give up your wallet with all your debit cards, credit cards and cash? What if you hand over the keys to your car and to your home and tell them they can have both? What if you invite them into a nearby store and go to the changing rooms to exchange outfits. Removing your nice clothes and shoes, you pass them under the door and exchange them for an old coat, some boots that don't match, and a shopping bag of assorted shirts, socks, gloves and hats. Finally, you take the cup of coins and head back into the cold to settle on the spot they previously occupied. You wave as the disbelieving panhandlers drive away in your car.

God could just have tossed us some of his wealth like so many coins in a beggar's cup, and that would have been generous. Instead, he traded places with us. Through Jesus, he stripped off his godly robes and wrapped them around our shoulders. Through Jesus, the father welcomes us into his eternal home. Through his son, the creator of the universe washed the filth of our sins from our hearts. Through Christ, he placed his Spirit within us and restored our joy. In our sin, we couldn't even articulate what we needed, and we longed for whatever he might give us out of pity. But he gave us everything he had and now we are rich!

To save us from our meager and meaningless lives, he had to trade places with us. He had to take our place of poverty. He lowered himself to our helpless position, took on the pain and death of our flesh and blood, wore our old tattered clothes of condemnation, and carried the burden of our sin as if it were his own. There he is, not crouching on a street corner, but hanging on a cross, taking our place, being punished for our sin. We stare in disbelief as we consider this incredible gift. He became poor so we could become rich through his death, burial, and resurrection. It's not fair. It's grace.

An old preaching hero of mine, Wally Rendel, used a lot of acrostics to explain deep Bible truths. The one he had for grace has stuck with me for almost thirty years. It is what today's teaching is all about. "Grace," he used to say, is "**God's Riches At Christ's Expense**." Paul says it is the grace of our Lord Jesus Christ that caused him to trade places with you and me while we were poor. This is beyond generous. It is extravagant; and once again we see just how much the God of the universe values us. Meditate on this and thank God for making you rich through Christ's poverty.

DAY TWENTY-TWO - INVEST

Matthew 25:15-18

"To one he gave five talents, to another two, to another one, to each according to his ability. Then he went away. He who had received he five talents went at once and traded with them, and he made five talents more. So also, he who had the two talents made two talents more. But he who had received the one talent went and dug in the ground and hid his master's money."

There is an old preacher's story about a father who wanted to teach his young son about giving. So before heading to church one Sunday morning, the dad gave his son both a quarter and a dime with the instructions that during the offering time, he was to give one to God and keep the other for himself. Later, the family piled into the car after the services and the curious father asked his son what he had given. Proudly, the youngster replied, "Well, before church I decided the best thing would be to give God the quarter and keep the dime for myself." The father smiled, pleased at his son's choice, until the little one continued, "But right before they passed the plate, the teacher said, 'God loves a cheerful giver.' I figured I could give a dime way more cheerfully than a quarter, so that's what I did."

This story provides both a humorous and convicting message concerning our attitudes towards giving. It also perfectly parallels the story Jesus told his followers 2,000 years ago to illustrate the stewardship call God has given each of us. Jesus' story tells of a master (who represents God) calling three of his servants (who represent us) to entrust to them large but differing amounts of money. The amount in this story would have grabbed the attention of Jesus' peasant audience. A "talent" of money in the first century was the equivalent of a common laborer's wage for twenty years. In light of this, we can make two conclusions about this master: he is super wealthy, and he is incredibly generous. This master is entrusting to three common household servants more money than they had ever seen or could ever earn in a lifetime. I could go on about the greatness of the master represented in this story, but today I want to focus on four investing lessons from this story.

Invest.

The first lesson is that the master intends for us to invest. The money you have right now, no matter how much you have or how you have gotten it, is from God. And God wants you to do something with it. In our verses, the good servants "went at once and traded with them." The word translated "traded" (*ergadzomai*) is more accurately translated "put his money to work" in the New International Version. You can probably recognize our current work-related word "ergonomic" from this ancient term.

The meaning of this word indicates that the good servants immediately went into business as investors. They may have opened a shop. They may have traded and invested in the market. They may have bought and flipped property. We don't know the details, but we know that they invested the master's money through work. They teach us that God has not blessed us with money so that we can spend it on ourselves. If he had, the master in Jesus' story would have said, "Here's some cash; go have some fun with your friends." On the other hand, neither has God blessed us with money for us to be timid and hold onto it for fear of losing it. If he had, the master in Jesus' story would not have condemned the servant who said, "I was afraid, and I went and hid your talent in the ground." (Matthew 25:25). All that we have is to be invested.

Invest for the master.

Specifically, our money is to be invested for the master to increase his kingdom. The surprising insight from this story is that God doesn't just want his money back. The master's wealth in the story speaks of incredible riches (move over Solomon and Bill Gates) and points to our God who literally owns everything there is. He is not interested in receiving back from us what he already owns in the first place. The point of the story is not that the master needs or wants more money. He is not using the servants to make himself richer. He is including the servants so that they can participate in his riches.

This means we are servants of a beautiful God who gives to us from his plentiful supply of riches so that he can involve us in investing his riches throughout the world. Because everything in the world is at his disposal, he can (and miraculously sometimes does) literally provide money and resources to meet any need, anywhere, at any time. But most often he has entrusted money to us so that we can put it to work for him. In this way, his kingdom increases, and we get to be part of the increase. Today, think of your God-given wealth. Whether it is $10 or $100,000 or $1,000,000; how can you participate in the master's work by investing your money to advance his kingdom through whatever cause he has called you to?

Invest according to your ability.

The next lesson is that God has different expectations for each of us. It's God who has the expectations, not us. The master (again, God) knew the capability of each of his servants, so he entrusts different amounts "to each according to his ability." The question is not who gives more for God or who has more to give. Have you ever thought that maybe you have the amount of money you have because God knows how much money you can handle? Is it possible that the "self-made" men and women who are successful at business are successful because God knew they would be and so entrusted more to them? Is it also possible that some good Christians will never have much wealth because God knows that more money could overwhelm them?

Obviously, I'm oversimplifying multiple variables that may affect our individual finances and wealth. But the encouragement is that God knows what you have, and he knows the ability you have to invest it. You simply can't mess up investing in the kingdom. God has given YOU the ability to do what he wants YOU to do with the resources he has given YOU. The master is not surprised when he hears that two servants have double what he gave them, but he was not happy that the third did nothing. The third servant had the same capability to succeed but he failed.

Invest for joy.

In the end of this story, the master (Jesus) tells the two who put his money to work, "well done faithful servant...enter into the joy of your master." Joy is not in the new car. Joy is not in the latest tech toy or gadget. Joy is not retiring with millions. A bigger house, newer trendy clothes, and trips to exotic destinations will not bring you joy. There is no joy in more. You will not find joy in possessions. No one—no one—has ever told me that the joy of their life is their money or the things they have bought with their money. Where will you find joy? According to Jesus, the greatest joy in this life comes from stewarding the money God has given us to increase his kingdom and his glory. It's true that he will someday return and welcome his faithful servants into his eternal kingdom, but we don't need to wait until his return. He has invited us to invest in his kingdom now. Let's put the money he has given us to work.

DAY TWENTY-THREE - FOOLISH INVESTMENT

Luke 12:18-21

"And he said, 'I will do this: I will tear down my barns and build larger ones, and there I will store all my grain and my goods. And I will say to my soul, 'Soul, you have ample good laid up for many years; relax, eat, drink, be merry.' But God said to him, 'Fool! This night your soul will be required of you, and things you have prepared, whose will they be?' So is the one who lays up treasure for himself and is not rich toward God."

What do you plan to do with all the money? This is the first interview question that is asked when someone wins the lottery. Often this question is met with a blank stare as the still-in-shock, instant millionaire mumbles the words, "I don't know; I still can't believe I won. I haven't had time to think about it." Other winners know exactly what they are going to do with the sudden windfall. They intend to go on a spending spree and they begin ticking off a dream list of immediate purchases: new house, new car, new wardrobe, and a trip around the world. The immediate purchase of the expensive things the winners never thought they could afford is a typical reaction to having more money than they ever imagined. But there are more conservative approaches to riches.

Some who hit the jackpot show a remarkable sense of frugality as they share their plans for their sudden prosperity. These people reveal that they will use their winnings to pay off debt, create a college fund for their kids, invest in a business venture, or save for retirement. A few of these contestants actually continue in their current careers, stay in their current homes, and continue to live the lifestyle they now enjoy. Except for pictures of them holding a giant check, you'd never know they had won the lottery.

If saving and investing for the future is wise, then giving the winnings away is generous. There are a few extremely benevolent winners. Some share their winnings with family and friends. They buy their parents a house, give their siblings large monetary gifts, or buy something extravagant for their friends. Others have a charity that is near and dear to their heart and so they bless a children's organization, a hospital, or an orphanage overseas. Then there are those who say, "First, I'm going to tithe to my church." I'm not making this up; I've heard it, and it secretly is every pastor's prayer, "Lord let a generous congregant win millions in the lottery." I'm just kidding. I have never prayed that prayer in my life and I don't use the word congregant to refer to the members of my church family. Seriously though, if you win, call me.

So, what would you do with more money than you could possibly spend? It is an interesting question and one that is asked in a story Jesus told 2,000 years ago. Remember, Jesus told the story right after he warned his followers to "...be on your guard against all kinds of covetousness" (Luke 12:15). As we've learned through this study, the desire for more money and all it can buy is an obstacle to Christ following. So Jesus tells a story of an already rich farmer (we should see ourselves as the rich man in this story based on our wealth compared to most of the world) whose land "produces plentifully." You know the saying, the "rich get richer"? Well in this story, this man does. He already had barns, but even they couldn't hold his bumper crop. In the story, he asks himself the question that each of us must ask. "What shall I do?"

Whether we win the lottery, earn millions, receive an unexpected inheritance, have a high yield on an investment, or have a great crop, what shall we do with the money? Maybe you're older and you have lots of money. What shall you do? Maybe you're a student and have nothing, but if you ever do, what shall you do? Maybe you're in midlife and you have a great plan for saving and retirement. What shall you do? Maybe you're early in your career and you don't think you have any extra money, but it's likely that even you have more than you truly need right now. So, what shall we do with our money? Ultimately, there are only three things you can do with any amount of money that you'll ever have in your life. You can spend it, save it, or give it away. Let's consider each of these choices through the lens of this Jesus story.

1. **You can spend it on or invest it in yourself.** This is the "I" part of this parable. Jesus tells it to help us understand our battle against covetousness. Notice that this rich man uses the pronoun "I" six times as he debates the options of his increased wealth. Aside from the fact that he is talking to himself, his selfishness is evident. Like the man in this parable, if we convince ourselves that all of our money, all of the time, is for us, we are simply being selfish. And I can tell you this with certainty: it is never acceptable for Christ followers to have this attitude towards wealth. God's verdict on selfishness? "Fool!"

2. **You can save it.** This man's solution was to save all of his extra income in bigger barns. I believe that there is good biblical endorsement for saving money. One of the best stories in the Bible is of Joseph saving for seven years to prepare for a worldwide famine. There is great wisdom in saving and in not spending all you have today. This practice is rare in our debt-ridden culture. However, our motive for saving can be selfish. The motivation for this man was so that he could "take life easy, eat, drink and be merry." Saving is good, but not if your goal is to get yourself to a life of "ease" and "comfort." What are you saving for?

3. **You can give it away.** The other option would have been for this man to give all of his extra abundance away. Instead of talking to himself, he should have prayed, asking God, "What shall I do?" and acknowledged that God made the field fertile and the crops plentiful. Within this scenario, he had a chance to give freely to others what had freely been given to him. This rich man had a chance to reflect the generosity of God to needy people around him. Think of the widows, orphans, and under-resourced people whose lives he could have changed; and he would still have been rich! Ultimately, this is the blessing and obligation of wealth for

all of us who call Jesus Lord. Like Abraham in Genesis 12, we have been blessed to be a blessing. How much can you give away? The more you give, the "richer toward God" (Luke 12:21) you are because in giving, you become more like him.

As Christ followers, these three options are the constant tension of stewardship. Like the rich man, we will all have money to steward throughout our lives. It's from God. Covetousness is a reality. Don't be foolish.

DAY TWENTY-FOUR - INVEST IN ONE ANOTHER

Acts 2:44-46

"And all who believed were together and had all things in common. And they were selling their possessions and belongings and distributing the proceeds to all, as any had need. And day by day, attending the temple together and breaking bread in their homes, they received their food with glad and generous hearts..."

From an early age I have experienced the love of the Church through the generosity of her people. When I was a kid living in poverty in Indianapolis, there were many times that my family and I would leave an evening worship service and find that someone had left bags of groceries in our car. Then as a young youth pastor (and still poor), my wife and I often received thank-you cards with a fifty-dollar bill inside and a simple encouraging note telling us to enjoy an evening out together. When we were still young in our ministry and marriage, we moved from Florida to the Midwest. With all of our travel expenses, and after closing on our first home (which was radically discounted by a Christian builder), we had $67 dollars to our names and two weeks until we were to receive our first pay check. But when we arrived to unload the rental truck, we discovered that our cabinets and refrigerator had been completely stocked with food. The church that we had not even begun serving had blessed us more than they would ever know.

I could tell a thousand stories from my thirty-four years of ministry about witnessing the generosity *of* the people of God *to* the people of God. I am still regularly blessed by the thoughtful generosity of the people we serve with, and now that we're in a different life stage, Sara and I try to bless others in the way that we have been blessed. In the last year, with our unborn grandson's chronic kidney failure and subsequent birth, our church has astounded me with ongoing generosity toward my son and daughter-in-law. There have been cards, prayers, lawn mowing, money, gas cards, gift cards, groceries, and more as the church has met the needs of my family in a way I can never repay. So through tears, I hug my kids and choke out the words, "Do you understand why I love Jesus' church so much?"

At its best, the church meets the practical everyday needs of its members. This generosity toward one another is firmly in the DNA of the church. The Christian community is designed to invest in one another, as we read from the early history of the church recorded in the book of Acts. They were devoted to "the fellowship," a phrase that implies common investment. The word "koinonia" was a first-century Greek word used most often to describe business partners—people who were equally sacrificial, invested in, and caring for the enterprise they were a part of. The church borrowed this word to describe the kind of relationship we have within the community of faith. As a fellowship of Christ followers, we are equally invested *in* one other and *with* one another. We are in this together and this means we care greatly not only for the spiritual growth, but also for the physical needs of our family members.

In today's verses, the word "common" is the root word for "koinonia." This commonality led some believers to sell their possessions and belongings. Both of these words may indicate land or property, as we see illustrated in the life of Barnabas two chapters later (Acts 4:37). After selling land or items, the proceeds were then "distributed" (a word that literally meant cut into pieces) to those in the church who had need. As I think about this story of the early church, I'm reminded of two things that are essential for this kind of fellowship to work.

Christian brothers and sisters must let others know of their needs.

We can assume that one of the major needs then was the same as it is now—food. This is why we have a food pantry (actually two) in our church. We know that there are many in our fellowship who cannot afford the food that is required to feed their families. So the food we gather is primarily for the Christian brothers and sisters within our fellowship. Though we hope and pray that we can fully eliminate hunger in our town, our first responsibility is to our spiritual family. This preference for the poor, the widows, and the orphans goes back to the Old Testament. If you study the context of each Old Testament command, God talks about caring for the poor people of God. Simply stated, there is no fellowship if members of the fellowship go without their practical and daily needs being met. The church really is a partnership.

Note that there is responsibility on the part of family members who have needs to let others know. If we are to be in true partnership for the gospel, then you are obligated to let me know when you have a need. This is hard in our culture where we all want to be self-made, self-sufficient, and independent, but the church is designed to have its members be dependent on one another. I have talked with brothers and sisters who have told me that they are embarrassed to use the food pantry. Don't be embarrassed. The joy of the fellowship is helping others in our fellowship.

Maybe you don't need food. Maybe you need help with an unexpected car or medical expense. Maybe you need transportation to the doctor, money for a son or daughter's sports league, help with some home repairs, or new clothes for your children. There are many things you may need today, but your Christian family will never know that unless you tell them. Can we become a fellowship who willingly, honestly, and humbly shares our needs with one another? Over my years of ministry, I have learned that there are hundreds who not only are able, but who sincerely want to help. But they can't help unless they know of your need.

Christian brothers or sisters who can should contribute to meet needs of others.

The other part of this fellowship of giving is to contribute, when you can, in a variety of ways. Do you know that every time you give to the church's general fund you are meeting needs? You are paying pastor and staff salaries, buying supplies for children's ministry, and supporting overseas ministries financially. As we will discover tomorrow, this support is expected from all church members. Additionally, we can contribute to all-church emphases like food-drive Sundays, seasonal projects (for us at Eastview this includes Imagine and The Serve Project), and expanding ministry offerings for under-resourced partners locally, nationally, and worldwide. More personally, we should contribute to our Christian family in small ways as God makes us aware of specific needs. What needs are you aware of in your closest fellowship circles? Pay attention and when you see an opportunity, meet that need with joy.

The result of all this "need meeting" in the church is described beautifully in our verse today. When we foster a community where needs are shared and met, we become a place where we are "together" with "glad and generous hearts." Do you have a need? Share it. Do you have something to contribute? Share it. Start today; we're in this together.

DAY TWENTY-FIVE - INVEST IN GOD'S HOUSE

Malachi 3:8-10

"Will man rob God? Yet you are robbing me. But you say, 'how are we robbing you?' In your tithes and contributions. You are cursed the with a curse, for you are robbing me, the whole nation of you. Bring the full tithe into the storehouse, that there may be food in my house. And thereby put me to the test, says the Lord of hosts, if I will not open the windows of heaven for you and pour down for you a blessing until there is no more need."

There is a long history of unbiblical explanations through the centuries when it comes to what we call "tithes and offerings." Just one example will make my point. In the Middle Ages, the church created an incentive for parishioners to give money by selling "indulgences." This was a payment to bribe your way out of your sins in order to avoid the judgment to follow in eternity. In those days, every church had an offering box called a "coffer" where people would drop their coins as they entered for worship. This explains a famous saying attributed to a 15th century German priest that goes, "As soon a coin in the coffer rings, the soul from purgatory springs." There is far too much bad theology in this jingle for me to explain it here. But church teachings like this and others that are equally wrong have caused confusion as to what offerings in the church are all about.

Yet, in most church services, there is an appeal to give to God by giving to the church. This "offering" takes many forms. Typically silver and gold trays have been passed down the rows of the sanctuary so that worshippers could place money in them. In frontier America, when fancy offering trays weren't available, a hat or plate was often passed which is why the sayings, "pass the plate" and "pass the hat" still mean that an offering is being taken. Many churches have eliminated this part of the service by putting offering boxes somewhere in the worship center. And written checks and cash are becoming obsolete as many choose to give electronically online through a church app or at a giving kiosk.

"Taking an offering" has been part of most worship services for nearly 2000 years of church history, and that's not going to go away. Why? Because even though some church leaders have abused, misspent and misappropriated the money the faithful have given, Christ followers are still commanded to be givers. So how should we give? How much should we give? Who should we give to? What does God require of us when it comes to offerings? Today's teaching helps us answer these questions as we see God's actual words about tithes and contributions (some Bible versions use the word offerings). For those who may be new to church, you may wonder what is meant by the "tithe." It is the Hebrew word (mah ah sayr) for a "tenth," the percentage that God required as the standard for what his people were to give to him. For the Old Testament people of God, there was no ambiguity in this law. Ten percent of your flocks, herds, cattle, grain, oil, wine, income, and anything else you could divide by ten belonged to God. Jesus even mentions how specific this practice became when he points out that the self-righteous Pharisees actually tithed the garden herbs mint, dill, and cumin (see Matthew 23:23).

The habit of many now is to ignore today's verses from Malachi as Old Testament requirements that no longer apply to those of us under the new covenant of Jesus' grace. But to do this is to misunderstand that God's entire, life-giving word does not change from testament to testament. Let's look again at what God thinks about tithes and offerings.

Bring them to my house.

In the Malachi passage, the house of God was the temple in Jerusalem. Before that, around 1,500 BC to 1,000 BC, the house of God was an ornate tent called the Tabernacle. The tithes of the people that Malachi references were used to support sacred practices in the house of God. There, the tithes provided oil for the lamps, wine and livestock for the sacrifices and food for the priests, grain for making the bread for the table in the Holy Place, and meals for those who served in the temple. The offerings given to God's house were both practical and sacred. I do not have space in this chapter to give a full biblical explanation of why I believe the church of Jesus is equivalent to the house of God mentioned in Malachi. My case is compelling, and I offer Ephesians 2:19 as the short version. In that verse, the apostle writes, "So then you are no longer strangers and aliens, but you are fellow citizens with the saints and members of the **household of God.**" Because the church is the household of God, we are called to give to support that household for both sacred and practical needs. This means that the goldfish crackers in the nursery are just as essential as the money sent to missionaries. Anything given to the church is given to God and furthers his mission in the world.

Don't steal from me by not giving.

All that we have learned here means that we are still obligated to give a tithe to the church. Some of us may not like the word tithe, pointing to the fact that the New Testament releases us from the confines of the law and that we live under grace. This is true, but the Bible reminds us that the grace of Jesus calls us to a higher commitment than the Law. "Thou shalt not murder" becomes "Do not hate others." "Thou shalt not commit adultery" becomes "Do not lust." So "Bring a tithe into my house" would certainly not become something less than 10% in Jesus' New Testament kingdom. Some would contend that the tithe is only a starting place and should increase as we mature. At any rate, whatever case we try to make for not tithing because we are under grace is a very weak argument. The truth remains—if you are not giving a tithe to God's church, you are stealing from him (his words, not mine). There are many who rationalize their lack of tithing to the church. They cite the grace of Jesus or complain about financial abuse committed by church leaders or remember a personal example where they felt their contributions were poorly used. None of these excuses are grounds for any of us to withhold tithes and offerings. We **owe God** a tenth of what he has given us.

There is blessing in giving tithes and offerings.

Think about how God must feel when he gives us everything we have, and yet we balk at giving ten percent back to him. If I offered you $10,000 every year on the condition that you give $1,000 away annually, you'd take that deal, right? I would. These verses give us another glimpse into the heart of God as he says to us, "If you give a tenth of what I've blessed you with back to my house, I will continue to bless you." How gracious is God! Yet I have met many who say, "I can't afford to give God ten percent of my income." But look again at today's verses; God actually challenges us to test him on his offer of blessing. I can personally testify that in 34 years of giving ten percent and more of my income, I have never gone without. So I'd say to you, "You can't afford *not* to give ten percent to God because he blesses that." And no, tithing isn't an investment we make so that God is obligated to give us more money, but you cannot out-give God and I've learned that if you trust God and give him what he has asked of you, he truly will take care of the rest.

Take some time to talk to God with honesty and humility about how much you are currently giving to his house. Are you robbing God? Is He pleased with what you are giving? Are you giving a tithe? Why or why not? Can you increase your giving? Why would or wouldn't you? Do you need to grow in your giving? How can you do that? These are intense questions, but the Bible *is* the word of God, and we must take Malachi 3 very seriously. I pray you do that today.

DAY TWENTY-SIX - INVEST GENEROUSLY

II Corinthians 9:6

"The point is this: whoever sows sparingly will also reap sparingly, and whoever sows bountifully will also reap bountifully."

I once heard a story about an early 20th century evangelist whose ministry included leading a church, holding month-long tent revivals, feeding and teaching children in the city, and training other preachers. The story goes that a ministry donor was impressed with all the spiritual and social outreach he had witnessed. He approached the preacher and asked, "How much ministry could you do with $1,000?" The benefactor expected the preacher to be impressed at the possibility of receiving such a generous donation. He thought that surely the preacher would exclaim over the donation and begin to list all the things that could be done in the name of Christ and in his ministry with such a large sum of money. Instead, the preacher barely glanced the man's way and replied, "About a thousand dollars' worth." So, how much ministry can be done with a thousand dollars? About a thousand dollars' worth of ministry. I love this story, because in my thirty-four years of ministry I've found that it's true.

One of the annual and necessary things we do at Eastview is create a working budget for the upcoming year. This months-long, extensive process doesn't begin with our accounting and finance pastors as you might expect. It begins with the input of each of our staff ministry teams as they come up with their proposals for doing God's work over the next year. These strategic plans, birthed in prayer and visionary leadership, put into writing what each ministry department hopes to accomplish for Jesus and his church in the upcoming year. These plans describe the programs to be created or supported, potential additional staff hires, the materials needed for equipping, and finally, the request for the financial resources to do all of these things.

When we collect all of these plans, we have dozens of proposals full of exciting ministry possibilities. Our gifted staff puts forth effective ideas, but every year many excellent programs are not pursued. And each year, staff positions go unfilled. Every year our facilities show a little more wear and pastors are not granted ministry money that they would use wisely. Why? Because a thousand dollars will only allow you to do a thousand dollars' worth of ministry. While our budget is far more than one thousand dollars, it is remarkable how much money we *don't* have for furthering the Kingdom. The bottom line is that if more money were given, the gospel could go forward even more powerfully, and God could use us to answer far more prayers. The amount of money given to our church directly affects the amount of ministry that can be accomplished. This is the giving principle that Paul is teaching the Christians in first century Corinth as he encourages them to give.

In today's verses, Paul was asking them to give generously to a special offering for the saints in Jerusalem who were experiencing a prolonged famine and suffering extreme poverty as a result. A year earlier, prompted by the Holy Spirit, this apostle had anticipated the need, and led by the Spirit, had taken up an offering from other churches to minister to needy brothers and sisters. So, as Paul continued his worldwide church-planting tour, he was collecting money for this ministry cause and appealing to the people in Corinth to be prepared to give generously when he arrived. Why was he asking them to give more? Because more money equaled more ministry in the Jerusalem church. Paul's message to that particular church family is still true today: "The more seed you sow, the more harvest you will reap."

The principle that is so obvious in the agricultural world is also true in the spiritual world of the church. The more money (seed) that is sown into the fields of ministry, the greater the results will be in advancing Jesus' kingdom. For the church, both then and now, the inspired, written word of God encourages us to participate in this great harvest of souls by sowing more in order to reap more.

Sow more.

There is no doubt that Paul was challenging the Corinthian church to sow more money than they had planned to give. He was asking them to take a step of faith: that's what sowing is. The sower scatters seed in faith hoping that God will cause his church to grow as a result. But our giving, our sowing seed, is a risky business. As illustrated by Jesus in his famous parable of the sower and the seed (Matthew 13:18ff), there are many conditions that can keep even a healthy seed from growing. Shallow soil, rocky soil, and thorns are just a few hindrances to a plant as it grows. In the same way, giving to the local church (or any kingdom cause for that matter) does not come with a guarantee. As sowers, we cannot predict or cause growth; only God can do that (I Corinthians 3:7). But we can sow generously.

At Eastview, we have just completed what I believe is the most generous sowing of seed in our sixty-four-year history. Over the first six months of 2019, we have gave the amount that was our previous monthly mortgage payment to bless six of our ministry partners locally, domestically, and worldwide. This means that in addition to our usual generous financial support for outreach, we have scattered the seeds of over half a million dollars in the name of Jesus! We believe that these seeds will reap thousands of souls for God over the next few years. And what I believe is true for the church, I believe is also true for each one of us. The more generously I give, the greater the potential is for growth in my own life and in my corner of God's kingdom.

Reap more.

The prayer behind all of this generous sowing is that we will see an increase in our harvest. I'll add a word of caution here about harvesting–if we're not careful we can manipulate this principle into an exercise of self-reward. Some have taught the concept that if you give $10,000 away, God will give you $100,000 in return. But the Bible teaches that sowing and reaping in the kingdom is not about growing our bottom line; it's about growing God's kingdom. The harvest Paul is talking about here does not result in a new car or home for those who are generous givers. Instead he says that believers who sow generously will reap a bounty of grace and salvation in their lives.

As we close, consider how much you are sowing and reaping. Today's verses leave no doubt that there is a direct correlation between these two things. So, to put it another way, "How much ministry can be done with the amount you currently give to the church?" Would you like it to be more? Decide today to start sowing generously because the more you sow, the more you'll reap.

DAY TWENTY-SEVEN - INVEST REGULARLY

I Corinthians 16:1-3

"Now concerning the collection for the saints: as I directed the churches of Galatia, so you also are to do. On the first day of every week, each of you is to put something aside and store it up, as he may prosper, so that there will be no collecting when I come. And when I arrive, I will send those whom you accredit by letter to carry your gift to Jerusalem."

One of my favorite family preaching legacies that no one cares about has to do with what Bible college students call "weekend ministries." A weekend ministry is a practical way for small churches who can't afford full-time pastors to fill their pulpit each Sunday with students who are learning how to deliver God's word. This is where the Baker legacy comes in. My father, my son, and I all had weekend ministries in Kentucky while we were students at Johnson Bible College (now Johnson University). My dad, Bob, preached at a church in Pittsburg, KY in the 1960's; I preached at Mt. Victory Christian Church in Mt. Victory, Kentucky in the 1980's; and Caleb preached in Harlan, Kentucky around 2010 (at Pansy Christian Church of all things). All of our experiences were similar, except when it came to how and when offerings were received. This gets us to our verse for today that seems to infer a weekly offering at First Christian Church of Corinth (which was not in Kentucky).

In the experiences that Caleb and I had, the offering was taken weekly in the traditional way by passing plates during the services. As I recall, the church I served had very little to support—a few missionaries, the monthly electric bill, an annual church picnic, and a weekly check to me for $75. My son's situation was similar, but he had a nice parsonage next to the church that was an extra bonus. These small churches (25 would be in the pews on a good Sunday) blessed young preachers as much as they could. For my mom and dad, their weekly payment came mostly in chickens, eggs, pies, and canned vegetables. On weekends, they stayed with a widowed matriarch of the church who was very hospitable, even though there was no running water in her house and the bathroom was an outhouse. Their monetary compensation was handled differently than it was for my son and me because that church really had only one offering a year. Yes, they passed the plate every week, but that habit didn't typically net more than some change or a small bill. This was because the congregation was made up almost entirely of tobacco farmers, whose payday came once a year—at harvest time. So, the church's support came from one large, annual offering.

In the first century church, we really don't know exactly how they collected offerings, but we know that they did. As we discussed on Day 24, the early church members invested in one another by "distributing the proceeds to all" (Acts 2:45), and we can assume that someone was in charge of collecting and disbursing the funds. On Day 31, we'll discover that those in the church also brought money and laid it at the Apostles' feet (Acts 4:35), trusting them to steward the church's gifts. As we read our verses for today from Paul's letter to the Corinthian church, we can infer that an offering was part of the weekly worship experience. There is strong biblical evidence that the church met on the "first day of the week" (our Sunday) and it makes sense that this is the day they would bring their offerings. We don't know exactly when offering and offering plates became part of the Sunday church experience, but even without the historical details, Paul's giving principles include instructions for an offering to be taken on Sundays. He writes to the Corinthians that offerings should be a regular investment for each believer.

The offering mentioned here is the same one we learned about yesterday. It was the special gift that Paul collected to give to the struggling

Jerusalem Christians who were suffering through a famine. I love the practicality of his instruction. He was hoping for a huge one-time gift, and he advised the leaders of the Corinthian church to accomplish this goal through a system of consistent giving week-by-week. The two simple rules for Christian giving listed below still apply for all who want to invest in the eternal kingdom of God through the church.

Rule #1 – Give regularly.

The first practical step Paul encouraged was for these early Christians to give regularly. Since they gathered weekly as a body to break bread, fellowship, pray, and hear the apostles' teaching, it made sense to take up a weekly offering. Regular giving is just as necessary in the 21st century because it helps pay for the week-to-week ministry of the church you attend. It would not take long for your church to be ineffective if members didn't give faithfully. But giving regularly isn't just about paying the church's bills. I believe it is also a spiritual discipline that moves us closer to the image of the God we serve. Think about it. How often does God give? Daily, right? The Bible says, "Every good and perfect gift is from above, coming down from the Father of lights...." (James 1:17)

Every good thing in our world today is a gift from God. This means that giving is a tangible way for us to be more like our heavenly father. Every time we give, we look a little more like our Lord. This means that there should be a consistent and predictable flow from your bank account to the work of the church through offerings. Take some time right now to think about your giving. How often do you give? Why have you chosen this pattern of giving? Is it enough? These are personal questions that each believer and every family must answer as the Spirit leads. As you consider how often you give, there is another helpful step.

Rule #2 – Give systematically.

The second practical step is to develop a system for giving: a plan. When it comes to giving, the system is easy to determine. Your system for giving is to be based on how you "may prosper." If Paul were writing this letter today, he might say, "...depending on how much money you make." He knew that the socio-economic make-up of the Corinthian church included slaves, merchants, craftsmen, wealthy landowners, and government officials. Each of these groups had different incomes and some had inconsistent incomes (e.g., an artisan who had a bad week of tent sales). But giving to God is never about the amount you give, but rather how much you give when compared to what you have been given. Your offering should depend on how you have prospered and that is different for each of us.

The other part of your system for giving is that each of us is to put something aside. Notice that Paul doesn't tell them a specific percentage to put aside. I have already shared that I believe the tithe is the place we begin, but that is a personal spiritual decision. What I do know, and the point I think Paul is alluding to here, is that if you don't have a plan (or system) in place for giving, it is likely that you will not give at all, or that you will give far less than your financial potential would allow. With today's technology, you can set a system in place that makes your offering automatic as you give online or directly from your bank account. Whatever method we use to give, it is important that we are realistic about our potential for giving and then that we set aside a carefully considered amount for God and his kingdom work. Evaluate your giving. Do you have a plan? If not, prayerfully make one that is within your means, and then stick to it. How much do you intend to give out of what God has given you? If you are already a systematic giver, when is the last time you thought about the amount you give? Maybe you could give more than you currently do. Set aside some time today to think about regular and systematic giving and whatever you decide to do, make your final plan based on faith.

DAY TWENTY-EIGHT - ETERNALLY INVESTED

Isaiah 55:1

"Come, everyone who thirsts, come to the waters; and he who has no money, come, buy and eat! Come buy wine and milk without price. Why do you spend your money for that which is not bread, and your labor for that which does not satisfy?"

We all like the sound of "free." This is why advertisers lure us to their services and products by offering free stuff. We are more likely to stay at a hotel that has "free coffee" or "free breakfast" included. We eat at restaurants where "kids eat free" and we have apps on our phone that reward us with "free drinks" for every five we buy. "Free admission?" We'll go. "Free vacation?" We'll listen to the sales pitch. "Free checking?" That's our bank. "First month free?" We'll rent that apartment. "Free miles?" We'll definitely fly that airline. "Pain free?" Let's go to that dentist. "Free puppies?" Look how cute. "Free upgrade?" Yes please. I could go on and on. We love "free." The problem is that most of the free things that are offered end up costing us something.

I could tell you a great story about a free pair of sun glasses that cost me $43, but I'll save that for another book. Actually, there is something for each of us that is truly free. It is the love of God and the offer to have what we are really looking for in life, from him, for free. In today's scripture, through the prophet Isaiah, we discover an invitation from God that truly costs us nothing. Four times in one verse God reveals his compassion for us through this simple invitation: "Come." This one word alone could be our devotional thought for the day—to grasp the reality that the God of all creation wants us to be close, to come near. Unbelievable! But the invitation he is extending is even more amazing than that. Through his son, Jesus Christ, he is offering us everything we long for, hope for, and pray for—completely free of charge. He is giving us a gift. To quote one of the most famous Bible verses, "The wages of sin is death, but the free gift of God is eternal life through Jesus Christ our Lord" (Romans 6:23).

The prophet points to all that we freely receive through Jesus by addressing our two great needs. We are all thirsty, looking for something that will quench our inner desire like a drink of cool water on a hot day. And we are all hungry, longing for something that will fill us like a good meal. Using these very human experiences as examples, Isaiah points to a God who will spiritually and deeply quench our thirst and our hunger by sending a Savior—his son Jesus.

Everyone is thirsty.

God points out that we spend much of our lives trying to quench our thirst with milk, wine, and water. This is true in the literal sense, but God uses this picture to illustrate our spiritual thirst. There is a deep-down soul thirst that we often try to quench through the world's options. Start with a tall glass of popularity. Drink up your self-image. Take a swig of fun. Chug some over-activity. Buy a six-pack of accomplishment. Yet still we thirst. We have "labored for that which does not satisfy" (v. 2). God says, "Come to me and I'll *give* you what you are working so hard to purchase." No money. No price. I freely give my son to quench your deepest thirst. Jesus says this to the woman at the well. "Everyone who drinks of this water will be thirsty again, but whoever drinks of the water that I will give him will never be thirsty again. The water that I give him will become in him a spring of water welling up to eternal life" (John 4:13-14). Jesus is this living water and by the grace of God, it is free. Drink up.

Everyone is hungry.

We're not just thirsty; we're also hungry. This is why "daily bread" is a part of the Lord's prayer and a major theme of the Bible. We need food every day, and without it, we experience the pangs of hunger. In the time of Jesus and the prophets (and even still in many places in the world), people either baked bread daily or went to the market to purchase enough for that day. In the same way, our souls hunger for nourishment and we need to pursue it every day. Unfortunately, we often settle for the menu offered by the world: the fast food drive-thru of sexuality for those hungry for love, and the junk food of bad relationships because we hunger for belonging. We over-indulge in everything from food to drugs because we hunger to feel good. Again, the question from God in our verse applies, "Why do you spend your money for that which is not bread?"

God has illustrated throughout Scripture that he wants to feed the hunger of his people. He put food in the garden for Adam and Eve. He rained down manna for his people in the wilderness. And Jesus fed thousands in the desert. All of this is a picture of the only food that will ever fill us and end our eternal hunger. His name is Jesus. Listen to his words: "Do not work for food that perishes, but for the food that endures to eternal life, which the Son of Man will give to you" (John 6:27). "I am the bread of life; whoever comes to me shall not hunger, and whoever believes in me shall never thirst" (John 6:35). Still today, the offer stands for us to come and partake of this living bread. In fact, we symbolically remember this truth every week by celebrating the broken body of Jesus as we take communion. Eat up.

Now and through eternity, God has invested in us so that we can experience something that is truly free. Because of his great love, there is something of incredible value that we need desperately and could never afford. But it's free! Near the end of the book of Revelation, the apostle John gives us a glimpse of our heavenly and eternal reality, and God's fulfillment of the "free" offer he made in Isaiah 55. Through Jesus Christ, to the very end of the Bible, the invitation remains—an invitation to the "free" we all long for.

"The Spirit and the Bride say, 'Come.' And let the one who hears say, 'Come.' And let the one who is thirsty come; let the one who desires take the water of life without price" (Revelation 22:17). The Greek word here that is translated *without price* is the word *dorean* and it indicates a free gift. So the words of Revelation 21:4, where we are promised no more tears, death, mourning or pain, and this offer for water without price, converge here. Tired of this world? Free forever. Tired of crying? Free of tears. Tired of hurting all over? Pain free. Tired of being thirsty? Free water. Tired of hunger pains? Free bread. Tired of regrets, sorrows, and past sins? Free from sin. How much would you pay for all of this? It doesn't matter because you couldn't afford it. But Jesus paid the price—and all of this is free. Yes please!

DAY TWENTY-NINE - WORSHIP

Matthew 26:7-10

"...a woman came up to him with an alabaster flask of very expensive ointment, and she poured it on his [Jesus'] head as he reclined at the table. And when the disciples saw it, they were indignant, saying, 'Why this waste? For this could have been sold for a large sum of money and given the to the poor.' But Jesus, aware of this, said to them, 'Why do you trouble the woman? For she has done a beautiful thing to me.'"

Most of us who are reading this book could probably describe worship based on our own personal church experiences. The most obvious expression of worship in these settings is often musical. Whether it's through participatory songs of praise or vocal and instrumental numbers offered by soloists, singing is the most common way most of us participate in public worship. It could be the old-school hymns accompanied by piano and organ, or modern songs accompanied by drums, fog, and moving lights (what a friend of mine calls "rock and roll church"). Either way, music is what first comes to mind when most us of hear the word "worship." Yet worship often encourages other biblical forms of expression like clapping and raising hands, shouts of praise, kneeling, standing, meditation, and even jumping.

Through the years, our worship pastor, Matt Ludwig, has taught us that music is only one form of worship. He uses the term "musical worship." Focusing only on music can cause us to miss other biblical and spiritual forms of expressing God's priority in our lives. One of these forms of worship is giving. From the stage we hear, "We are going to continue our worship by taking up our tithes and offerings," but the short prayer preceding and the announcements following seem to downplay the act of giving. This is why this book and this chapter are so important. Giving our money is not a methodical paying down of a debt we owe Jesus, or a way to buy his friendship. No. According to our verses from today, giving something of value to Jesus out of love, and from a sincere heart, is a beautiful act of worship.

Actually, the story Matthew recalls in chapter 26 is not a "traditional" worship experience at all. The setting is one of life's basic experiences: Jesus and his followers sit at the table enjoying dinner together in the home of a gracious host named Simon. And though it is just a meal, I would suggest that this dinner *was* a kind of worship service. Jesus is only days away from being crucified in Jerusalem. He is having dinner two miles away in a town called Bethany. It is Passover week, and like all faithful Jewish people, these dinner guests had likely been to the temple earlier that day. A spiritual anticipation is in the air. Even this meal, which featured unleavened bread, foreshadowed the first communion, with Christ himself sitting at the table. Naturally, they prayed the traditional blessing over bread and it's quite possible they sang together (see Matthew 26:30). We can also guess that Jesus was teaching as they ate and that others asked questions. So it's a meal, but in many ways it included the elements of a worship service, and one that had not been planned.

Unexpectedly, a woman appeared with an alabaster container of expensive, perfumed oil and anointed Jesus with it. This event is told with some variation in each of the gospels (see Mark 14:3, Luke 7:36, and John 12:1). These probably cover at least two separate events with different details given by each author. If you are interested, further personal study would help integrate these historic accounts, but our focus today is on the gift and the worship expressed in this woman's generosity. Today, as we consider giving as a form of worship, there are at least three components that made this woman's gift "a beautiful thing" in Jesus' eyes.

Give extravagantly.

There were many ways this woman could have expressed her worship of Jesus in this setting. She could literally have bowed at his feet in humble submission. She could have written a song or poem that expressed her truest feelings. Like the leper who returned to thank Jesus for his healing, she could simply have said, "Thank you, Lord." She might even have stood up and given her testimony of how Jesus had changed her life and then encouraged others to follow him. All of these acts would have been proper forms of worship for who Jesus was and for all that he had done for her. But she wanted to worship extravagantly.

She wanted everyone to witness and understand her complete devotion to Jesus. A woman coming this close to a man publicly would have been a stunning spectacle for first century sensibilities. But Jesus' followers had gotten used to his liberating welcome of women. Then there was the scent of worship. The apostle John notes, "The house was filled with the fragrance of the perfume" (John 12:3). Finally, we have the scene of the Christ, sitting at the table, anointed (and dripping) with expensive, perfumed oil. This is simply show-stopping giving. It was extravagant. When was the last time your giving could be classified as extravagant, and what would that look like now, in the 21st century?

Give it all.

Historically, these alabaster bottles from the first century were not intended to be reused. They did not come with tops or stoppers like our colognes and perfumes have. The container had to be broken to access the ointment inside. This meant that once the sealed neck of the bottle was fractured, all the valuable perfume had to be used. There was no partial use; it was all or nothing. Once it was open, the bottle had to be emptied. So, this woman poured the entire contents on Jesus.

Traditionally, many Christ followers have viewed the tithe (ten percent of one's income) as the end goal of giving to the church. But I would contend that the Christ-following life requires us to give more and more until we give everything. For many years, my wife Sara and I have worked hard at moving towards "all" and have moved our giving from 10% to about 17%. I'm not sure we'll ever get to the point of giving away 100% of our income, but I know this—if you don't intentionally plan to give more and more to Jesus over time, you'll never give as this woman did.

Focus on Jesus, not others.

There's one other brief impression left from this story. The woman seems completely unaware of the other guests sitting at the table. She seems to be focused on Jesus alone. As all eyes turned to the scene unfolding before them, this woman's eyes were locked on the object of her worship. Notice that other Christ followers questioned the woman's worshipful giving, asking, "Why this waste?" (v. 8). But all she cared about was honoring Jesus, and he responded that her giving was a beautiful form of worship. That should be our goal as well. Our giving should not be about what others think, or about what others expect, but only about what Jesus thinks. So, what *does* Jesus think of our giving? That's the focus. Think about this today: "How differently would I have to give to Jesus and his church for him to see my giving as a beautiful thing?"

DAY THIRTY - ALL IN WORSHIP

Luke 21:1-4

"Jesus looked up and saw the rich putting their gifts into the offering box, and he saw a poor widow put in two small copper coins. And he said, 'Truly, I tell you, this poor widow has put in more than all of them. For they all contributed out of their abundance, but she out of her poverty put in all she had to live on.'"

When listing our favorite life experiences together, Sara and I would include our times with about two hundred special and beautiful women in Central India. In our work with our ministry partners there, we have had several opportunities to meet, encourage, and give gifts to the widows from the towns surrounding the church. We are humbled by them. These women, many of whom have walked miles, arrive in groups with smiles on their faces and wearing brightly colored clothes. I'm moved by this because they live in a culture that sees them as cursed. Their position as widows is believed to be a judgement for something they have done, perhaps even in a former life. They have "bad Karma," their culture tells them. For this, and many other reasons, their prospects for remarriage and security are slim.

Because of their circumstances, these women find themselves near the bottom of their society's ladder and they live in extreme poverty. The last time we were there, we were told that these widows receive a two-dollar-a-month government stipend which is barely enough to keep them alive. Sara and I have been involved in distributions where we have had the privilege of giving each woman a two-pound bag of rice and a sari (a colorful Indian dress). As we kneel to greet them, Sara kisses every woman on the cheek, and both of us hug and hold hands with as many as possible. In those moments, it feels as if God is touching these women with his hands of love through us, even as he touches our hearts through them. I never leave those times with dry eyes, and I never read today's verses without thinking of the Indian widows.

The first century widow Jesus observed giving her offering at the temple was a lot like these twenty-first century Indian women. She too found herself the "least of these" in social standing. She lived in poverty. She, like them, probably received a distribution of food from the temple treasury as stipulated under Jewish law. She, like them, had next to nothing that she could truly call her own. And she, like the Indian widows, wouldn't be the one we'd expect to be praised for her capacity for giving. This is the why the story of this "poor widow" and her gift at the temple is so amazing. It's amazing that she gave something, but it's even more startling that Jesus said it was the best offering of the day. How could this be? The coins she dropped into the temple treasury that day were so insignificant it is likely that they didn't even make the traditional clinking sound that most coins would.

The coins we commonly refer to as a widow's mite were copper, minted by the Hasmonean King Alexander Jannaeus between 103-76 BC. Actually, to call this crude currency a coin is nearly an exaggeration. I own some of this 2,000-year-old currency and it would be more accurately described as thin chips of copper that have been individually and irregularly struck with a hammer. No two of them are alike. Some have the image stamped close to one edge of the metal, and some close to the other. I've seen some that only have half of the impression on the coin. By the time of Christ, they had been replaced by the Roman currency of talents and denarii, making the ancient coins of a long-ago deposed Jewish dynasty worth next to nothing. The coins this poor widow dropped into the offering on that day at the temple had almost no value. And yet, Jesus noticed. Why? What was it that caused Jesus to make such an extraordinary statement about her generosity? Consider for a few minutes…

Her gift was humble.

As we learned this past summer during our "Summer on the Mount" series from Matthew 6, giving at the temple could be quite a show. In that teaching, Jesus says that some donors actually announced their offerings with trumpets (Matthew 6:2), literally "tooting their own horns" so that others might notice their religious generosity. Not so with the widow. I picture her walking with a cane, inching slowly toward the treasury box with her coins in hand. Quietly, humbly, without others noticing, and with absolutely no fanfare, she gave God her small gift and moved away. She probably didn't even know that Jesus noticed her. Giving that is worship is humble.

Her gift was all that she had.

Even though this woman had next to nothing, she gave away all that she had. She didn't have a plan for how she would pay for bread the next day. She didn't have a job. She didn't have savings in some jar. She may not even have had a place to spend the night. But she gave everything she had anyway. Most of us will never give everything we have in an offering, and I'm not suggesting that we should. The call to stewardship is different for each servant. I do know, however, there is great joy in dedicating something completely to God through giving. We practice this at Eastview by praying individually for the miracle of a financial windfall each Christmas and then dedicating everything that God miraculously gives us to the Expanding Ministry Offering. There is no greater joy in worship than giving back to God the money you didn't have until he gave it to you. There is something incredibly worshipful about giving away ALL of something.

Her gift was an act of worship.

This biblical widow is our first example of what it means to worship with our resources. Throughout our time in this study, we've talked about giving to God because it shows what we **treasure**. We have learned to offer what we have to God because we highly **value** the kingdom of heaven. And we have been reminded that all we have has been given to us so that we can **invest** in his kingdom. But this widow shows us something greater, something deeper. Our resources, great or small, can be a tangible form of worship. Beyond the amount, and beyond what impresses others, we give a sincere offering from our hearts to the very heart of God. As the widow approached the treasury box with hundreds of other worshipers, she wasn't concerned about what others thought. She wasn't thinking about an amount that might impress God. She simply brought all she had to worship the one she loved more than anyone or anything else. Every time we give to Jesus and to his kingdom with all that we have, we are worshiping. Just as lifting our hands or clapping during a praise song or kneeling in reverence during prayer is worship, our giving is an act of worship. How can you worship through giving like this widow did?

DAY THIRTY-ONE - WORSHIP BY GIVING CREATIVELY

Acts 4:34-37

"...as many as were owners of lands or houses sold them and brought the proceeds of what was sold and laid it at the apostles fee, and it was distributed to each as any had need. Thus, Joseph, who was also called by the apostles Barnabas (which means son of encouragement), a Levite, a native of Cyprus, sold a field that belonged to him and brought the money and laid it at the apostles' feet."

It is amazing how imaginative church people can be when they are challenged to be creative so that they can give more. Throughout the years, I've seen this giving frenzy happen as we've raised money for capital campaigns and mission offerings. And I've seen us illustrate the parable of the talents from Matthew 25 as the church has offered money to each attendee, small group, or member, suggesting that they use it to generate more. Sometimes, people were encouraged to pool resources or to be creative with what they already had. Over and over, I have seen Christ followers put the resources, possessions, and gifts they have to work in some really remarkable ways.

Let me share what this can look like. Below is a *non*-comprehensive list of the innovative giving ideas I have witnessed and been blessed by throughout the years:

- Uber drivers have used seed money to buy gas and donated all their tips to the church.

- Students have chipped in to buy car wash supplies and raised hundreds of dollars through donations.

- A few guys rented a lawn aerator and went through their neighborhood charging people to get their lawn ready for summer.

- One lady bought ingredients to make cupcakes and sold them at her kids' school.

- Several church families combined for a massive garage sale and gave all the proceeds to a building program.

- One person offered a sports car that had been sitting in the garage, and another donated expensive artwork that had been in the basement for years.

- One man cashed in an old collection of coins and donated the proceeds to a mission trip.

- A couple downsized to a different home so that they could give thousands of dollars for a capital campaign at their church.

- People have sold baseball cards on eBay and clothes to a second-hand store.

- Math and English teachers have donated their time to tutor grade school children, giving the profits to the church.

- Businessmen have donated trucks for transporting supplies for our food pantry and shuttles to provide transportation to elderly church members.

- Families have donated land for ministry use or sale.

- People in the food industry have donated pizzas by the hundreds and ice cream bars by the thousands.

- A man with a motorcycle charged kids in his neighborhood a dollar a ride and donated everything to the church.

- A single mom who cuts and styles hair donated all of her tips for a month to a mission.

There are many more examples I could list, but you get the idea. Most Christ followers really work at giving offerings and tithes from their income. But there are ways to multiply our giving through means other than our income. When we think creatively, there are myriad ways we can turn our resources into more income for the kingdom, and generosity becomes a joyful form of worship.

This seems to be what was happening in the very first church in Jerusalem. The church was growing, the gospel was spreading, and the financial needs were increasing. So people like Barnabas started thinking, "Hey I've got a field I could sell and give the proceeds to the church." Imagine the joy when he came to the fellowship and announced that God had blessed his transaction with a large profit to help with the mission of the church. We don't know exactly how great the gift was, or how many people were blessed, or how the money was used. But we do have this story and I think it has been preserved in our scriptures so that we can learn from it. Consider three Barnabas lessons:

1. Take inventory of your possessions. Most of us, regardless of our income level, have items we no longer value, but that someone else would want. This is why we see garage sales everywhere. We should thank God for providing such an overabundance of possessions and then admit that we have many things that we don't need. What extra things do you have? Why not worship by selling them so that you can give more to the cause of Christ?

2. Pledge and pray. When you identify objects that you are willing to part with, dedicate them to God and ask him to bless your faith by multiplying these resources for his kingdom. Make sure you

follow through with your commitment. Don't try to lie to the Holy Spirit (See Acts 5:1-11 for details). Why not worship God in faith and trust? He has given you more so that you can give more.

3. Encourage others. Finally, I do not think it is any coincidence that the meaning of Barnabas' name, "son of encouragement," is a description of what he did through his gift. There is nothing as encouraging as giving sacrificially and "spurring on to love and good deeds" (Hebrews 10:24) through our own examples. Why not worship through creative giving by leading the way in your small group, your circle of friends, or your ministry team to find exciting ways to increase your offerings to the church?

These questions are not rhetorical; they are meant to be acted upon. So, what will you do in light of this great story from Acts?

DAY THIRTY-TWO - WORSHIP BY GIVING OFTEN

Leviticus 7:37&38

"This is the law of the burnt offering, of the grain offering, of the sin offering, of the guilt offering, of the ordination offering, and of the peace offering, which the Lord commanded Moses on Mount Sinai, on the day that he commanded the people of Israel to bring their offerings to the Lord, in the wilderness of Sinai."

When I was a teenager, my dad and I and about 40 other fathers and sons from our church traveled by bus from Indianapolis, Indiana, to Honobia, Oklahoma, for a gathering called the Kiamichi Men's Clinic. Kiamichi was an annual men's conference named after the mountain range in which it was located. It was known for rustic camping on forty acres with all day preaching, lots of worship, and male-focused spiritual formation. This was before the Promise Keeper's movement, and at the time, it was the largest Christian conference for men. Ten thousand attended annually.

On Thursday evening of this weeklong event, we would pile into buses and go to local small churches to have a meal, encourage the congregations, and worship. The churches we visited were scattered through the hills in an area that was heavily Native American. One worship service in particular stands out in my memory. With no air conditioning, a standing-room-only crowd of 500 men in a 300-seat sanctuary, and the heat index in the high nineties, we heard a great sermon. But the thing that made this night so memorable was the number of offerings taken and one very zealous elder's passionate appeals to give.

The first offering took place early in the service as we were asked to bless the humble brothers and sisters of the church, who were living in near-poverty conditions. The plate was passed, and men gave. As sermon time approached, this same elder returned to the microphone and interrupted the program. He chastised us for not giving generously enough and pleaded, with tears in his eyes and a raised voice (I'm not exaggerating here), for us to give more. Another hymn was sung as the offering plates were passed again. Believe it or not, after the sermon, the same man jumped back onto the platform and appealed AGAIN for us to give even more, and with that the volunteer ushers passed the offering plates one last time during the closing song. I never found out how much money was raised that evening, but I know that my teen-aged mind wondered just how many offerings there could be in one service.

According to our reading from today, apparently a lot more than three offerings were a standard part of worship in Old Testament times. In these verses, the six major offerings involved in worshiping God are summarized from the descriptions we are given in Leviticus 6. Each offering had different rules and was given for different reasons, but they were all part of the requirements for worshiping God. It was a complex system of giving, and time does not permit a full explanation, but below is a brief description of each offering to help us understand the giving required of the Israelite people.

- **Burnt offerings** were offerings to make atonement (Hebrew "ka phar" – to cover) for the sins of the people. These offerings were burned completely on the Altar of Burnt Offering and a further description can be found in Leviticus 1 & 6:8-13.

- **Grain offerings** were offerings that were given voluntarily to "memorialize" or acknowledge God. They came in the form of fried, baked, or boiled bread; or grains ground into meal. It was always seasoned and unleavened. For further description of this offering see Leviticus 2 & 6:14-18.

- **Ordination offerings** were offerings that were specifically given for ordaining Aaron and his sons for their service as priests. This indicated an offering from the priests who were normally given a portion of each offering for their daily needs. For more specifics see Leviticus 6:19-23.

- **Sin offerings** were offerings for specific sins that an individual or community had unintentionally committed. They were given as purification so that one could enter into the presence of God. Extensive rules for this offering are found in Leviticus 4:1-13 & 6:24-30.

- **Guilt offerings** were given by the people to make restitution for their offenses. Every sin, accidental or not, had a price attached to it, and this offering made it right with God. For further reading on this offering see Leviticus 5:14-19 & 7:1-10.

- **Peace offerings** were gifts given as tokens of thanksgiving to God, often eaten in unity and fellowship between two people, parties, or families (i.e., peace with God and man). You can learn more about this offering in Leviticus 7:11-36.

Yes, that was the short explanation! And there is more to the offering requirements. The six listed above do not include the annual offerings given during harvest and other seasons of the year, in addition to holidays and festivals of worship. Some scholars estimate that Jewish people in the Old Testament gave up to thirty-three percent of their income when all of the offerings were added up. What's the point? The point, then and now, is that there is simply no way to divorce worship of God from giving to God. God designed offerings to be given habitually, routinely, and consistently because he always wants us to be reminded that giving is a part of our God following life. The more we practice giving to God and his church, the more our hearts are inclined to worship him with our offerings.

DAY THIRTY-THREE - WORSHIP BY GIVING BEYOND

II Corinthians 8:1-4

*"We want you to know, brothers, about the grace of God that has been given among the churches of Macedonia, for in a severe test of affliction, their abundance of joy and their extreme poverty have overflowed in a wealth of generosity on their part. For they gave according to their means, as I can testify, and **beyond** their means, of their own accord, begging us earnestly for the favor of taking part in the relief of the saints..."*

"Tandewar" was the refrain of the worship song that moved me so deeply that morning. With great joy and energy, the thousand or so Christians gathered in Damoh Church, India, repeated, "Tandewar. Tandewar. Tandewar. Tandewar." It was a catchy tune and I started singing along, but what was I saying? I leaned over to my friend, Dr. Lall, and asked him for the meaning of this word. His reply was "Thank you. It is a song that is telling God how thankful we are for all the he has given us." This was the song my Indian brothers and sisters sang as they participated in their annual "Thanksgiving" offering. I had the privilege of preaching the sermon in that service, but it was the congregation that preached to me that day.

The tradition for this church is that once a year, in November, all the believers bring a special gift to the church to demonstrate their thankfulness for God's grace and provision in the previous year. But this offering is not the typical time of passing baskets up and down the rows to collect money. Instead, this yearly outpouring of generosity is a full-participation demonstration of gift-giving. Their offerings are brought forward and laid on the steps of the of the church's stage. It is a beautiful sight to behold, and I've witnessed wave after wave of joyful givers proceed to the front of the church with a gift as they sing "Tandewar". Even those whose dress and demeanor would indicate a life of poverty come forward in joy with fruits and vegetables from their gardens and even eggs from their henhouses to lay before God. As long as I live, this experience will be my mind's example of the Christian grace of worship through giving. It was joyful. It was earnest. It involved everyone. It was inspirational. It was giving that was "beyond" (v. 3).

Today's scripture commends New Testament congregations who were setting the example for giving and generosity in the first-century Christian world. Paul praises the grace exhibited in these churches in the northern region of Greece known as Macedonia. As we've seen in previous readings, he is actively collecting a special offering from all the churches to give relief and aid the church in Jerusalem. And in these verses, he encourages the wealthier believers in Corinth to follow the example of the Macedonian Christians in "this act of grace" (II Corinthians 8:7). Just like the Indian church mentioned above, these early Christians were giving "beyond" tithes, offerings, and even their means. Prayerfully, we will be challenged today to follow their example and become a fearless church of Christ followers who are known for worshiping God through our generosity. There are four components to this type of worshiping through giving.

Giving "beyond" is joy-filled.

In the ancient language of the New Testament (technically Koine Greek) the word "joy" is the root for "grace", "gift", and "gifts". A quick language lesson will help us understand the wordplay in these verses. "Joy" in verse two is the Greek word "xara" where the "x" is pronounced as a hard "ch" sound. "Joy" is also the root word of "grace" (Greek "xaris") found in verses one, six, and seven (also found in verse four translated as "favor" in the ESV). Then when we come to the word "gift" in verse three, it is the related Greek word "xarisma" from which we get the word "charisma." Why am I telling you this? Because joy, grace, and gifts are all wrapped into one. Joy-filled giving is an expression of grace. The grace of Jesus was the gift he gave us through his death on the cross; "for the joy that was set before him..." (Hebrews 12:2). The Macedonian church expressed the grace of Jesus through their joyful gifts. It is both the gift of grace and the grace of giving—and joy is literally in all of it. You will know that you are giving "beyond" because of the joy that fills your heart as you give.

Giving "beyond" is earnest participation.

Look at the attitude of the Macedonian church. They didn't say, "Oh no. Here comes the apostle looking for another handout." They literally begged to give. The word is "earnestly" in verse four and it indicates repeated appeals from these Christians to be allowed to give. They had already given before, but they sought the opportunity to give more. Paul didn't have to make another appeal or challenge them to give more. When he or his associates came to town, these believers begged to give. You will know that you are giving "beyond" when you are finding ways to give more.

Giving beyond what you have.

In the Jesus following life, giving is not limited by how much one does or does not have. Worshiping through giving means having the mindset of our ancient brothers and sisters who gave "beyond their means." You may think that this is impossible. How can I give more than I have? Isn't it irresponsible to give away more money than I need to have to live and support my family? Well, in regular economics it might be; but not if we learn to trust two things about God: 1) God blesses generosity, and 2) God will never run out. If we think of ourselves as conduits of his resources, we can give beyond our means because we are giving of *his* means. Our "bottom line" becomes insignificant because God has no "bottom line." You will know that you are giving "beyond" when you stop thinking of what you don't have to give and start focusing on what God has for you to give.

Giving beyond inspires others.

Can you imagine how this letter spurred its recipients to "love and good deeds" (Hebrews 10:24)? The church of Jesus is designed to be a community where we are inspired, and where we inspire faith in others. So, it's simple: when I see a brother or sister give sacrificially, I'm challenged to sacrifice as well. Our prayer is that the generosity of the Christ followers at Eastview will go viral, infecting every member of our congregation with generosity. Did you know that your giving can actually be contagious? Well, it can be. You will know that you are giving "beyond" when others are inspired by your giving.

DAY THIRTY-FOUR - WORSHIP BY GIVING EXCESSIVELY

Exodus 35:5

"Take from among you a contribution to the Lord. Whoever is of a generous heart, let him bring the Lord contribution…. And they came, everyone whose heart stirred him, and everyone whose spirit moved him, and brought the Lord's contribution to be used for the tent of meeting…. All the men and women, the people of Israel, whose heart moved them to bring anything for the work that the Lord had commanded by Moses to be done brought it as a freewill offering."

"Today before I begin my sermon, I'm going to ask you all to do something with your offerings that you may not believe. After a thorough review of all of our ministries, the elders have determined that we have plenty of space to expand and grow in our ministry and worship facilities for the next 20 years. All the carpet is new. The walls have fresh paint. All of the church's mechanical systems are new. The parking lot is freshly paved, and the building has recently been re-roofed. We are fully staffed; we have all the pastors we need, their ministries have more resources than they can spend, and they are all overpaid. Our vision to sponsor every child in Haiti, Kenya, and El Salvador is now a reality. There are no hungry or homeless people in our county and we have planted churches in every major city of the world. In light of all these realities, I'm announcing today that until further notice we will not be accepting any more tithes or offerings. You've got it right. We want you to stop giving. We have too much money for the work God has called us to." SAID NO PASTOR, EVER!

In a previous day's devotion, we talked about the cost of doing ministry; and noted that the more money you have, the more ministry you can do. Because this is true, I have never met a preaching pastor who is not aware of the expenses associated with ministry and the need for the gifts of God's people to pay for them. I'm certain there will never be a time (until Jesus returns!) when our church's tithes and offerings are no longer needed because the work of God has been completed. But the context of today's verses actually tell of a time when a congregation gave so abundantly they were told to stop giving. Exodus 36: 5 & 6 summarizes it this way: "The people bring much more than enough for doing the work that the Lord has commanded us to do. So Moses gave command, and word was proclaimed throughout the camp 'Let no man or woman do anything more for the contribution for the sanctuary.' So the people were *restrained from bringing* (emphasis mine)."

The contributions referred to in this instance in Jewish history were for the construction of the worship tent referred to as the Tabernacle. This dwelling, along with its courtyard, would be the place the Lord would dwell, his presence represented by a pillar of fire and a pillar of cloud. It would be located in the exact middle of the Israelite camp, so symbolically and in reality it would be the center of all worship and worship experiences. In light of this, God gave Moses exacting specifications for everything from the dimensions of the tent to the design of every piece of furniture to the bells and pomegranates decorating the hem of the High Priest's robe. God also chose, inspired, gifted, and called the two men who would be the lead craftsmen and designers for this project. Everything was in place except for the materials needed to construct such a worship facility. So Moses took up an offering. This was not just any offering—it was a campaign of donations for the Tabernacle that involved every man and woman of the people of Israel. They worshiped by excessive giving and their actions show us how we, too, can worship like this. What made these people give until they were told to stop?

They gave because of a heart condition.

I wonder if Moses did what many church leaders have done when proposing a building campaign. Did he host manna banquets and talk to people leader by leader, tent by tent, and tribe by tribe? Did he give a rousing speech about how God was doing a great work with them and through them for his purpose? Did he share salvation stories from the camp or remind them of how God had helped them in the past? We don't have any record of such tactics, but whatever he did, the people were moved. They were moved on the inside. They all had a heart condition that caused them to give like this. This offering required people with "generous hearts" (v. 5). This Old Testament outpouring of resources was from people whose hearts had stirred them (v. 21). These contributions came from "willing" hearts (v. 22).

What is your heart condition today? Are you excited about your church and the way God has used it to save you, grow you, and give you hope through Jesus? Are you moved by the way your congregation nurtures, raises, and matures future generations by ministering to the children and youth? Does your spirit stir within you when you see someone profess faith in Christ and be baptized? Do you have a generous heart? Are you convinced that the vision and mission of your church is advancing the kingdom of the king you serve? The kind of excessive giving we're talking about begins with this internal movement of the spirit within. Give as you have been inspired.

They all gave something.

Our verses for today, along with the entire account of this offering in Exodus 35, are filled with all-inclusive descriptions of who gave: "everyone," "every man," "all the women," "they all" brought some kind of contribution. Some brought olive oil, others brought gold, and still others brought handmade linen. But whatever the contribution, when the Tabernacle was finished, they could all worship there knowing that each of them had an investment in this great work. Unfortunately, the same cannot be said about most American churches.

126

The often-repeated 80/20 church giving ratio that I've heard all my life remains true. This giving statistic reveals that in most congregations, twenty percent of the members give eighty percent of the finances to fund the ministries of the church. Two questions come to mind as I consider this fact. How much work could be done in Jesus' name if 100 percent of God's people contributed generously all the time? How much joy are people missing out on when they see the miraculous, life-changing, eternal work of the kingdom and know that they didn't contribute anything to it?

Yes, I'm a dreamer, but I pray that this study will help us become a people who are so moved by the work of God that we all give, all we can, all the time until we have given so much we are told to stop. May God make us into a congregation who worship through excessive giving.

DAY THIRTY-FIVE - WORSHIP THE KING OF ALL RICHES

Romans 11:33-36

"Oh the depth of the riches and wisdom and knowledge of God! How unsearchable are his judgments and how inscrutable his ways! For who has known the mind of the Lord, or who has been his counselor? Or who has given a gift to him that he might be repaid? For from him and through him and to him are all things. To him be glory forever. Amen."

If you hang around church very long, you'll hear a lot of words that end in the suffix-"ology." This addition at the end of a word is derived from the word "logos" and means "word." Whenever you see this, it indicates a "word about" or "study of" the word it's attached to. For example, and perhaps best known, is the word *theology* which literally means "a word about God" (theos [God] + logos [word]). Similarly, *Christology* is "a word about Christ," and *eschatology* is "a word about escha." Just kidding; it's the study of the end times (Greek *eschatos* means "last"). Many of us have heard another word with this ending during a funeral service; the *eulogy* is literally a "good word" about the deceased. Okay, is this an English language lesson on word structure, or is there a point to all of this?

There is a point, and it's found in the word that describes our Scripture reading for today. The word is *doxology* and it means "a glory word" (*doxa* in Greek means "glory"). Depending on how you count them, there are about 28 doxologies in the New Testament. These are outbursts of prayer that give glory to God, sometimes at the end and sometimes in the middle of the sacred texts of our Bible. Because they express praise to God, doxologies can be the perfect ending to a worship service, a personal prayer time, or as in this case, a book called "Cost: The Price for Following Christ." In the introduction we noted, "No one paid a higher price for us to come close to God than God himself." So it is appropriate for us to end our study by giving him the praise that is due him.

Today we are going to approach our reading as more of a spiritual practice than a devotional thought. Together, we are going to use this doxology as a guide for prayer, slowly considering and personalizing lines from this benediction as we consider the cost one last time. With each line from this doxology, I will suggest two or three "cost" prayers, but feel free to follow the Spirit's leading into other prayers.

Oh, the depths of the riches and wisdom and knowledge of God!

- Praise God today for his inestimable wealth.

- Consider the stars, the ocean, endless fields, mountains, campfires, smiles, and perfectly formed children. Express to God your admiration for parts of his creation that feel overwhelming to you.

- Confess to God your limitations. Tell him how much money you're worth, how much wisdom and knowledge you have, and then acknowledge how small you are when compared to his glory.

Who has given a gift to him that he might be repaid?

- Acknowledge the gift of Jesus Christ and tell him how grateful you are that he gave us his son.

- Talk to God about how **valuable** Jesus is to you personally.

- Confess to God the ways in which riches have been or are an **obstacle** for your faith.

- Make a renewed commitment to God to give more, not to repay him, but to **worship** him.

For from him and through him and to him are all things.

- Think of ten of your most valued possessions and give them to God, acknowledging each as a gift from him.

- Commit to God what you would like to give him in light of this study. If all things are "to him," start by giving something of yours to him.

To him be glory forever. Amen

- Give glory to God for his riches.

- Give glory to God for entrusting some of his riches to you.

- Give glory to God for accepting offerings from you as a gift.

When I was a kid, there was a ritual that followed the taking of the offering in each service. After all the trays were passed and collected at the back of the sanctuary, the deacons would stack them and prepare to bring the gifts of the people to the front. On cue, the entire congregation would stand and sing "The Doxology" as these men carried our tithes and offerings forward where they were placed on the communion table. This was a tangible and visible way to express glory to God and give back to him at the same time. And I think this is a great way to end our journey together. Sing it or say it. But whatever you do, mean it.

Praise God from whom all blessings flow;
Praise Him all creatures here below;
Praise Him above, ye heavenly hosts:
Praise Father, Son, and Holy Ghost.

COST

Cost Study Guide—Introduction

We make choices every day; choices of all shapes and sizes. Some choices are well thought out, and others sneak up on us. Of all the choices in the world, there is none more important than choosing to follow Jesus. When we come face to face with determining who Jesus is, and then how we should live in light of knowing him, we are faced with a life-changing, transforming decision.

As we reflect upon and share our own stories of journeying toward Jesus, we are reminded of the demanding nature of following him. Jesus himself was very clear in Matthew 16:24 that anyone who wants to be his disciple must bear his own cross. This deliberation is both weighty and strengthening. We know the difference Jesus has, is, and will make in our lives. It's why we opened our hands, surrendered our ways, and gave it all to him. However, even as "full-fledged" Christ followers, on a daily basis we are faced with choices that reinforce or deny our professed follower-ship. There is a need for a daily remembrance of who we are figuratively, literally, mentally, physically, cognitively, and spiritually following.

Because of the importance of daily surrendering anything that flies in the face of Jesus, this five-week study will focus on Jesus' words in Matthew 16:24, "Then Jesus told his disciples, 'If anyone would come after me, let him deny himself and take up his cross and follow me.'"

In conjunction with the Sunday sermons and the 35-day devotional, this weekly study should challenge all of us to count the cost of following Jesus daily. In various ways, we will be encouraged to lean into a genuine, authentic Christ-following life.

Gather: This section can be used to get to know your group more fully. Whether you are a new group or an existing group, it's important to learn about each other.

Grow: This section focuses on the main teaching passage(s) for each week. In addition, your group will journey through other new and old testaments stories that correspond with each week's theme.

Give: This section will challenge each group member to count the cost of following Jesus with a weekly check-in exercise. Please take time to complete this section while your group gathers together.

Go: This section will encourage you and your group to live out each week's theme in your everyday life.

In addition to this study, there are more resources available at www.eastviewresources.com that can help you, your family, and your small group count the cost of following Jesus.

At the end of the day, there are a number of things that can keep us from fully following Jesus. We hope and pray that through this study, you will be encouraged and strengthened to give and live for him!

Thank you,

Jason Sniff
On Behalf of the Eastview Small Groups Team

COST STUDY GUIDE – WEEK ONE - OBSTACLE (GUT CHECK)

Days 1-7

Each of us faces huge obstacles when it comes to following Jesus. This week's study focuses on Matthew 19:16-30 and an interaction Jesus had with a rich young man. As we study and immerse ourselves in this passage and the daily devotionals for this week, let's reflect upon the obstacles that keep us from truly following Jesus.

Gather (your group getting to know each other)

If this is your first time gathering together as a group, take some time for group members to introduce themselves and talk about 2-3 unique things about their lives. Then use one of the following questions to start your group gathering:

- Describe a time you were confident you knew the right choice. How did it turn out?

- Talk about a financial decision you've made and any sacrifice(s) that decision brought.

If you've been together as a small group for a while, consider the following:

- What obstacles keep your group from gathering together on a consistent basis?

Grow (your group counting the cost)

- Open the group in prayer. Ask specifically that God will reveal any areas of life we keep as our own.

- If your group meets later in the week, review and discuss the daily devotionals you've read. If your group meets earlier in the week, peruse and capture the main ideas of each day.

- Watch the "Obstacle" video and write down any phrases that stand out.

_____

_____

_____

_____

- Read Matthew 19:16-30 as a group and discuss the following questions:

    o In your own opinion, why did the rich young man walk away?

    o Jesus gave two responses to the rich young man that both start with the word "If." What can we learn from his answers?

    o Daniel Doriani says, "Clearly this man wants to know what he owes God. Better yet, what can he do so that God is obligated to him."

- If we are not careful, all of our relationships can be reduced to transactional, tit for tat relationships; "What's my return on investment?" How does this attitude creep in to our relationships with other people?

- If we are honest, what checklists or transactional rules have we created in our relationship with Jesus?

- What does Jesus reveal about his kingdom in verse 30?

- There is another instance in the gospel accounts where Jesus challenged someone to count the cost. Read the story of Zacchaeus found in Luke 19:1-10 and compare his response to the rich young man.

- Through the course of this study we will look at the life of King Solomon. As he took over the kingdom from his father, we learn of a unique interaction where God basically says, "Ask for anything you want and I will give it to you." Solomon asked for wisdom. Read 1 Kings 3:10-14.

  o Take note of God's responses to Solomon.

  o What is the commitment that God asks of Solomon?

  o How is Solomon asked to count the cost?

  o How has Jesus asked you to walk in his ways, and keep his statutes?

- Discuss the two takeaways mentioned in the Day 1 devotional:

  o "Disciples will always give up something to follow Jesus."

- Why is sacrifice seemingly synonymous with following Jesus?

- What sacrifices have you / do you make as a Christ follower?

o "With God all things are possible"

- Recall the times that God has done that which seemed impossible.

- Days 5 & 6 devotionals instruct us that real satisfaction and contentment do not come from money or a desire for wealth.

Ecclesiastes 5:10: "He who loves money will not be satisfied with money, nor he who loves wealth with his income; this also is vanity."

Hebrews 13:5: "Keep your life free from the love of money, and be content with what you have, for he has said, 'I will never leave you nor forsake you.'"

- We all approach money differently. What is it about money that particularly gets in your way of fully trusting Jesus? When has Jesus been enough for you?

Give (your group serving and loving each other)

- In light of Mike's second step in the teaching video, answer the question, "What do you still lack when it comes to fully following Jesus?" If you are really brave, ask your spouse and/or a trusted friend what they think you still lack.

- As we read Matthew 19, we are left thinking that the biggest obstacle for the rich young man was his trust in wealth over his trust in God. He ended up turning away from Jesus and toward the comfort of his wealth. For each of us, obstacles come in all shapes, sizes, and disguises. At the end of the day, however, an obstacle is anything that keeps us from fully trusting in Jesus with all of our life.

------------**Gut Check**-----------

"If anyone would **come after me**, let him deny himself and take up his cross and follow me."
Matthew 16:24

If we are to follow Jesus, we need to examine our obstacles. Take some time and write out the obstacles that keep you from fully going after Jesus. Examples could include safety, power, control, comfort, approval, beauty, serving others, wealth, materialism, individualism, legalism, moralism, political ideologies, addictions of all kinds (work included), doctrinal errors and selfishness. The list could be long; but share your list with the group as time allows.

- _____
- _____
- _____
- _____
- _____
- _____
- _____

Go (your group living this week on mission)

- Continue reading the daily devotionals. Week 2 covers days 8-14.

- As we count the cost this week, Mike challenged all of us during the teaching video to, "go, sell, give, and follow." Over the next four weeks each of us is encouraged to participate in a "Barnabas Challenge." Literally, find something of great personal value, sell it, and give the earnings just like Barnabas did in Acts 4:36-37. At the end of this Cost study we will have a time to celebrate and to give away the earnings from this formative act.

- Be sure to utilize the www.globalrichlist.com resource Mike mentions in the video teaching.

- For additional resources consider Tim Keller's book, "Counterfeit God: The Empty Promises of Money, Sex, and Power, and the Only Hope that Matters."

COST STUDY GUIDE – WEEK TWO - TREASURE (HEART CHECK)

Days 8-14

This teaching from Jesus' sermon on the mount will help us understand where our treasure is located. In Jesus' economy, there are two places you can invest your resources; earthly treasures or heavenly treasures. During this study we will be challenged to determine where our heart lies between those two opportunities for investment. Whether your heart follows what you treasure, or what you treasure follows your heart; this will be a heart check for us.

Gather (your group getting to know each other)

- This is not a joke; Which comes first, the chicken or the egg?

- In the same vein; Is leadership innate, or taught and caught?

Grow (your group counting the cost)

- Open the group in prayer, asking specifically for God to reveal what we truly desire in life.

- Spend some time reviewing, perusing, and discussing the daily devotionals.

- Watch the "Treasure" video and write down any phrases that standout.

_____

_____

_____

_____

- Read Matthew 6:19-24 as a group and discuss the following questions:

    o As you look at this passage, what is happening? What is the context of this passage? Who is this passage for?

    o What can we learn from Jesus' teachings about our treasures, our eyes, and who or what we place at the center of our lives? Take each part of the passage and really squeeze out, and interpret as much as you can.

    o Now that we've observed this passage and its various parts, and have taken time to learn and interpret Jesus' teachings, how then should we rearrange our actions to live by his words? Based upon this passage, how will you live this week?

- Jesus uses treasure language in other teachings and parables. Take a look at Matthew 12:33-37: in particular verse 35. What is Jesus saying to the Pharisees and people around him?

- As we follow the life of King Solomon, 1 Kings 6 provides us with another milestone in his God-following life. As he began building the temple, God asks Solomon to count the cost:

"Concerning this house that you are building, if you will walk in my statutes and obey my rules and keep all my commandments and walk in them, then I will establish my word with you, which I spoke to David your father. And I will dwell among the children of Israel and will not forsake my people Israel." (1 Kings 6:12-13)

- What is God asking of Solomon? What key words or phrases help with your answers?

- What does God promise?

- How does Solomon respond?

- When it comes to treasures and our heart, the Day 8 devotional gives us three important questions. If you haven't already done this, take time to answer the following truthfully:

  o Time: What do you treasure with your time?

  o Talent: What do you treasure with your talent?

  o Money: How are you spending your money?

- As we consider storing our treasures in heaven, a practical question of "how" rises to the top. Mike talked about how we can do this in the teaching video. Daniel Doriani affirms this, saying, "We store up treasures in heaven by giving generously of them on earth." Tim Keller supports this from the opposite direction, saying, "Greed and materialism blind us spiritually." Read out loud Psalm 112:1-5 and Proverbs 11:24-26. How can we store up treasures in heaven?

Give (your group serving and loving)

```
------------Heart Check------------

"If anyone would come after me, let him deny
himself and take up his cross and follow me."
Matthew 16:24
```

Jesus calls all his people to examine their hearts, to be completely honest about who or what is at the center. IF we are going to count the cost of followership, we will do well to examine all the areas of our life that entice us away from him.

What is it that we fret about most?

- _____
- _____
- _____

Apart from our loved ones, what or whom do we most dread losing?

- _____
- _____
- _____

What is it that we believe we cannot be happy without?

- _____
- _____
- _____

What is it about money that allures you the most?

- _____
- _____
- _____

Where is your heart?

- _____
- _____
- _____

Go (your group living this week on mission)

- Continue reading the daily devotionals. Week 3 covers days 15-21.

- Share the Matthew 6 story with friends and let them know how you are being challenged.

- One of the ways to store up treasure in heaven is to be purposeful in using your time, talents, and treasures to bless someone else.

  o As an individual and as a group, commit to the holy habit of blessing those you know. Who has a tangible need? Be specific; actively pursue others in their need, and watch what Jesus does through this habit of blessing.

  o If you are not already aware of a need, pray that God would open your eyes to see and fill the needs of someone else.

COST STUDY GUIDE – WEEK THREE - VALUE (PRICE CHECK)

Days 15-21

Beginning with the phrase, "…the kingdom of heaven is like…" Jesus tells two very short parables that speak to value. In each story, a person finds something. In each, the person who makes the discovery sells everything in order to purchase the discovered treasure. Like the pearl and the treasure, every Christ follower has claimed and valued Jesus by faith and become a part of his kingdom. But how much do we truly value Jesus? This week's study will help us price check how much we value our Lord and Savior.

Gather (your group getting to know each other)

- What is the most expensive thing you've ever purchased? (or since everyone may say "my house" perhaps amend this to "you've purchased in the last year")

- If money were no object, what is one thing you'd purchase for yourself?

Grow (your group counting the cost)

- Open the group in prayer, asking specifically for God to reveal what you value most in life.

- Watch the "Value" video and write down any phrases that stand out.

  _____

  _____

  _____

  _____

- Read Matthew 13:44-46 as a group and discuss the following:

  o What does this passage teach us about Jesus?

  o How do you determine what is worthwhile in life?

  o What is worth risking everything for?

- In the midst of gathering, calling and sending out the twelve disciples, Jesus tells a story about the value he places on them and us. Read Matthew 10:29-33. What kind of value does Jesus place on us? What other verses remind you of how much Jesus values us?

- Paul talks at great length about finding the value of following Christ and gives examples from his own life about placing Jesus above every other thing. As a group read Philippians 3:8-14. How does Paul value Jesus? How does he challenge us to value Jesus?

- It took seven years for Solomon to complete the building of the Lord's temple. He then led the nation of Israel through a dedication ceremony. During this sacred occasion, he prayed specifically for all of Israel to value God. As a group read 1 Kings 8:54-61. Take particular note of verses 58 and 61.

  o What was Solomon urging Israel to value?

  o How did Solomon instruct Israel to value this?

- o What might have gotten in the way of Israel living out these instructions?

- In the Day 15 devotional we are reminded that "the kingdom of God is the most valuable thing there is," and "the great value of the kingdom is worth great sacrifice to get it." We are faced with three questions worth discussing as a group:

  - o If you follow Jesus, do you value him like the treasure and the pearl?

  - o If you follow Jesus, how have you valued him in your life, wealth, and service?

  - o If God put a literal, monetary price tag on human salvation, how much would you pay for yourself? Your family? Your friends? For strangers?

- What other points in the daily devotionals challenged you this week?

- Jesus uses a pearl and a treasure to describe himself and his kingdom. What words or valuable things would you use to describe him?

Give (your group serving and loving each other)

------------**Price Check**------------

"If anyone would come after me, let him deny himself and **take up his cross** and follow me."
Matthew 16:24

Every Christ follower is faced with surrendering his own will and desires and then Jesus tells us how to obey. We are instructed, literally, to pick up and take upon ourselves the cross; the ultimate evidence of the value we profess in following Jesus. In the teaching video, Mike said that all of us are looking for four things of value: love, purpose, belonging, and forgiveness. For each of these values, determine what you need to take up and give to Jesus.

Love:

_____
_____
_____
_____

Purpose:

_____
_____
_____
_____

Belonging:

_____
_____
_____
_____

Forgiveness:

_____
_____
_____
_____

Go (your group living this week on mission)

- Continue reading the daily devotionals. Week 4 covers days 22-28.

- Take some time and share with a valued friend how Christ is moving you closer to him.

- One of the ways we can value Jesus is by valuing his people. Hospitality is a deeply spiritual, holy habit and an attitude that values those he came to serve. When we open our homes and invite people to eat with us, we acknowledge that value. This week, actively seek others who may or may not be Christ followers and invite them to your dinner table. Demonstrate their value through a good meal and conversation together.

COST STUDY GUIDE– WEEK FOUR - INVEST (TRUST CHECK)

Days 22-28

This week's study is based upon Jesus' famous parable about the talents. A master gives various amounts of talents (money) to three different servants and entrusts them to use these talents wisely. It's a parable about faithfulness and stewardship and how each servant invested what he was given to increase the kingdom. God (the master) has given each of us (his servants) resources to steward for his name and for his kingdom. Can God trust us to be faithful to invest all that he has given us, or are we fearfully clinging to what we have? Are we faithfully or fearfully investing our talent(s)?

Gather (your group getting to know each other)

- When you receive a monetary gift are you more apt to spend it quickly or to save it?

- What have been some unwise uses of your time, talents, or treasures in the past?

Grow (your group counting the cost)

- Open the group in prayer, asking specifically for God to reveal how you are to invest your most valued resources.

- Watch the "Invest" video and write down any phrases that stand out.

  _____

  _____

  _____

  _____

- Read Matthew 25:14-30 as a group.

  o   As we look at the parable of the talents, take a few minutes and work through the following three questions.

  ▪   What do we learn about Jesus in the passage?

      _____

      _____

      _____

  ▪   What does this passage mean?

      _____

      _____

      _____

  ▪   What must I do to obey?

      •   I will . . . .

      •   I will . . . .

o   In the midst of his fear, the last servant chose a course of action that didn't end well. When it comes to following Jesus, where might we be afraid and what are the results of that fear?

_____

_____

_____

o   Within the context of this passage, what does verse 29 convey?

_____

_____

_____

• In the very next section of scripture, Jesus drives home the theme of kingdom investment. He provides another tangible parable about what it means to be a true follower and steward his resources. Read together Matthew 25:31-40.

o   What are the are six ways the "sheep" faithfully invested in the kingdom?

_____

_____

_____

o   Who are the brothers and sisters referred to in this passage?

_____

_____

_____

o   How can your group steward your resources in a similar fashion?

_____

_____

_____

• After Solomon finished building the temple and his own house, God appears to him just as he had in 1 Kings 3. Here, God lays out an investment strategy for Solomon. Read 1 Kings 9:4-9 as a group.

o   What does God say will be a good and faithful investment for Solomon?

_____

_____

_____

o   What will result from an unwise investment by Solomon?

_____

_____

_____

o   King Solomon warned us about some of his unwise investments. As time permits, read Ecclesiastes 2:10-11. How do Solomon's teachings relate to our lives, even now?

_____

_____

_____

- In the Day 22 devotional we are encouraged to invest in three ways:

    o Invest for the master. What has Jesus entrusted to you to invest in his kingdom?

    _____

    _____

    _____

    o Invest according to your ability. According to who you are, your gifts, your abilities and circumstances, how can you invest in his kingdom?

    _____

    _____

    _____

    o Invest for joy. How can you give joyfully?

    _____

    _____

    _____

- Review this week's daily devotionals. What passages impacted your thinking about the theme of invest?

    _____

    _____

    _____

- It's been said that following Jesus is not a passive way of life. As followers we are called to activate and capitalize on every opportunity. Even in the midst of fear; when we use our talents, the kingdom advances. As you consider your world and your circles of influence, o   Where are the places you can serve?

_____

_____

_____

o   Who are the people you can serve?

_____

_____

_____

o   What are the things (time, talent, money) you have to offer
as you serve?

_____

_____

_____

Give (your group serving and loving each other)

-----------**Trust Check**-----------

"If anyone would come after me, let him deny
himself and take up his cross and **follow me**."
Matthew 16:24

One of the main reasons the third servant didn't invest his talent was
because he didn't trust his master. Driven by mistrust, he assumed the
worst and acted accordingly. Trust is a major component of following
Jesus.

o   If you are completely honest, where might you be squandering opportunities to use your time, talents, and money for the kingdom out of fear or mistrust?

o   In what areas of your life do you not fully trust Jesus?

Go (your group living this week on mission)

- Continue reading the daily devotionals. Week 5 covers days 29-35.

- One of the best ways to learn to trust Jesus is to spend time listening to and learning about him. Listening is a holy habit that creates space to quiet the noise, eliminate the busyness, and open our minds and hearts to hear him. A quiet heart is our best defense against fear and mistrust. Designate 15-30 minutes of uninterrupted time each day this week and let Jesus reveal any fears and lack of trust that are lurking underneath the surface. Pray that he will remove them from your heart and mind.

COST STUDY GUIDE – WEEK FIVE - WORSHIP (BLANK CHECK)

Days 29-35

This final week's study will look at two opposite ends of the cost spectrum. At one end, Judas betrays Jesus for 30 pieces of silver and at the other, Mary worships Jesus with an extravagant jar of precious ointment. The dichotomy between their heart-motivation is remarkable. So is the decision we are called to make to follow Jesus; either for what is in it for us, or to love him enough to pour all we have at his feet.

Gather (your group getting to know each other)

- What has been the most expensive gift you have given? Who was it for and for what occasion?

- What is the best gift you've ever received?

Grow (your group counting the cost)

- Open the group in prayer, asking specifically for God to reveal how you can worship through your giving.

- Watch the "Worship" video and write down any phrases that stand out.

  _____

  _____

  _____

  _____

- Read Matthew 26:6-16 and 27:3-8 as a group.

  o Place yourself in this story. Of all the people represented in the passages, who do you naturally relate to the most? Who would you have the hardest time relating to?

  o Compare the jar of perfume and the 30 pieces of silver. What do they represent about the heart worship of each person?

  o Why were Jesus' own followers indignant about Mary's gift? Have you ever found yourself critical of another person's decision to give without knowing the full story?

  o What can we learn from Jesus' two "for" statements?

  o How can giving be worship?

- Mark 12:41-44 records a story about the worship-filled giving from a widow. In it, Jesus talks about the idea of abundance.

  o What is the difference between giving from abundance and abundantly giving?

  o Has there been a time where you sacrificially gave all that you had?

  o Do you live out of a mindset of scarcity or abundance?

- Following Jesus is a whole-hearted, worship-filled adventure. Through the years, however, King Solomon's heart began to worship things other than God. 1 Kings 11:1-10 captures the disheartening end of his journey.

    o According to the passage, what led to Solomon's disobedience? Take note of repeated words and phrases.

    o If this kind of sad ending can happen to the wisest person on earth, what should we learn from this passage?

    o If left unchecked, what things will eventually betray your heart's worship of Jesus?

- The Day 29 devotional encourages us to give extravagantly, completely, and intentionally. Consider the following:

    o Are you a calculated giver or an extravagant giver?

    o What is Jesus worth to you?

    o Does (How might) your everyday life demonstrate Jesus' worth?

- In the midst of a record-setting fishing adventure, Peter, James, and John count the cost and choose to follow Jesus. Read Luke 5:3-10.

    o In particular, note Peter's interactions with Jesus in verse 5, and 8.

    o Describe what happens in the hearts of these three disciples.

    o How do they worship Jesus? If you were in that situation, would you do the same?

- Review the daily devotionals. Which one stood out the most for you?

Give (your group serving and loving each other)

> -----------**Blank Check**-----------
>
> "If anyone would come after me, let him deny himself and take up his cross and **follow me.**"
> Matthew 16:24

As we continue to follow him, Jesus calls each of us to consider deeply who we will worship. Worship isn't just an experience, but also an outward expression of our heart desires. Take some time and authentically examine the following:

- What do you care about most in life? Be honest.

- What parts of your life do you worshipfully and extravagantly pour out?

- Is there anything that you cling to; that you clutch?

Go (your group living this week on mission)

- Finish the daily devotionals and reflect upon your daily journey over the past 35 days. What devotions were the most challenging?

- When it comes to money, how will you live differently after having gone through this study? Are there certain habits that you are going to change or add?

- It's been said that truly following Jesus costs us our plans and our expectations, but that the exchange is worth it. If we are serious about following Jesus, then knowing who he's created us to be helps us worship him with everything we have.

  o Take some time this week and go to www.freeshapetest.com to learn how you are created to serve, give, and to worship extravagantly.

Printed in the United States
By Bookmasters